Readers Theatre
in Rhyme
A Collection of Scripted Folktales

Readers Theatre in Rhyme
A Collection of Scripted Folktales

By Winn Braun and Carl Braun
Illustrated by Winn Braun

PORTAGE & MAIN PRESS

Layout and design by Relish Design Studio Ltd.

Printed in Canada

Library and Archives Canada Cataloguing in Publication

Braun, Carl
Readers' theatre in rhyme : a collection of scripted folktales /
Carl Braun and Winn Braun.

Target audience: For grades 3-7.
ISBN 1-55379-072-3

1. Readers' theater. 2. Readers (Elementary) 3. Children's plays.
4. Children's poetry. I. Braun, Win, 1959- II. Title.

PE1119.B7325 2005   428.6   C2005-906075-1

PORTAGE & MAIN PRESS
100-318 McDermot Avenue
Winnipeg, Manitoba, Canada R3A 0A2
E-mail: books@portageandmainpress.com
Tel: 204-987-3500
Toll Free: 1-800-667-9673
Fax: 1-866-734-8477

Contents

Bumbling Silliness

Tales of Trespass

That Rocky Road to Happiness

Lovingly dedicated to

Tyler Epp, a young man with language sophistication, imagination,
and a touch of arcane humour far beyond his years.

Matthew Braun, whose quiet reflections around stories run deeper than words.

Mikala Epp, whose love of language and brilliant sparkle marks
the reading of every poem or story as a celebration.

Phillip Braun, whose insatiable appetite for story and verse can
never quite be satisfied — the days are simply not long enough!

Acknowledgements

Our joy in seeing children and adults involved in Readers Theatre has only grown over the twenty years since we first discovered the ways it can be used in and out of the classroom. We have observed readers across the literacy spectrum from floundering to fluent, from turned-off to tuned in, and from emergent and second-language readers to older readers all reaping the rewards of the non-threatening, supportive environment that Readers Theatre offers and encourages. We thank the many children who have immersed themselves in this magical piece of the literacy pie. Their enthusiasm for going beyond the words on the page has encouraged us to venture into yet another Readers Theatre project. We also thank the many teachers and parents who have celebrated with the children, giving to all the opportunity for the success and joy of literacy.

We would especially like to thank Mikala Epp and Pat Hogan for their incredible support and critical ears, as together we read the scripts aloud. Thank you also to Tyler Epp for his insightful, and sometimes humourous grade-seven perspective on vocabulary choice in various scripts.

Grateful acknowledgement is also made for permission to retell and script: "Little Urban Riding Girl," by Reece Bennett, a grade six student from Matheson Island, Manitoba, permission granted by Cam Giavedoni, Superintendent, Frontier School Division, Manitoba, on behalf of Reece's parents.

INTRODUCTION

Readers Theatre in Language Learning and Instruction

Readers Theatre: Its Place in Classroom Learning

Readers Theatre is a collaborative or shared reading of a poem, story, or the lyrics of a favourite song. Above everything else, Readers Theatre is an interactive medium for the presentation of a piece that doesn't have to be memorized. While pieces are scripted, ready to read, and readers are assigned to particular roles, Readers Theatre also leaves scope and flexibility that invites students and teachers to improvise. It can be adapted to virtually any situation. Some students may want to design and use costumes while others may feel that the voice is enough to paint pictures for their audience. The fact that Readers Theatre doesn't come with a prescription may be one reason that teachers and students quickly become hooked. They can create on their own terms, and what one class may achieve with a script may be dramatically different from another class. The following scripts are meant to spark creative twists as you, your students, and others give free rein to your collective imagination.

How often to use Readers Theatre

How often to use Readers Theatre is an individual decision made by each teacher. Some teachers plan it as a fun activity on Friday afternoons as a diversion, while others incorporate it into their daily timetables. While Readers Theatre offers excellent diversion potential, it would be wrong to view its value so narrowly. We suggest using Readers Theatre often throughout the year. The process is productive for students and offers a joyful opportunity for performance in the classroom, for special occasions and school functions. It provides an excellent means for integration in language arts and social studies. How frequently Readers Theatre is used often depends on students who have generally had wide exposure to it and love it. Students begin to suggest occasions for Readers Theatre celebrations. When this happens, you can be sure Readers Theatre has become its own teacher.

For educators, Readers Theatre has another attraction. It is an oral engagement. Children hear the oral, they produce the oral, and since they are engaged in scripts that require practice to achieve fluency, the strings of language, nuances, structures, embellishments, and rhythms all become part of the emerging intellectual and linguistic landscape of the mind. Readers Theatre is an avenue through which students learn language, learn through language, and learn about language.

Readers Theatre has the potential to improve the learning and instructional environment. It invites, even demands, cooperation between students and teachers so the learning enterprise can shape and re-shape routines in creative and caring ways. As Eisner suggests: "… although good teaching uses routines, it is seldom routine … it depends on sensibility and imagination … it courts surprise … it profits from caring … good teaching is an artistic affair." (Eisner, 2002, p. 77) Readers Theatre allows teachers and students to tap into their creative potential, and they have fun at the same time.

About the Scripts

The scripts in this latest Readers Theatre book are based on tales from many different cultural traditions. We hope that apart from the pleasure of reading students will garner some appreciation for the folktale tradition, and its universal appeal in portraying beliefs, superstitions, and customs. Through these scripts, we offer a small taste of at least some of the universal themes that transcend folktales in many cultures. For example, there are three versions (of the more than 1500!) of the

Cinderella story – the well-known German Grimm's version, a Chinese version, and a Canadian First Nation version. The story of little red riding hood, with a modern twist, is based on the story written by Reece Bennett, a grade 6 student.

Bettleheim (1977) viewed tales as central to providing children with insights into dealing with life's problems directly and without compromise:

> The deeper inner conflicts originating in our primitive drives and violent emotions are all denied in much of modern literature, and so the child is not helped in coping with them…The fairy tale, by contrast, takes these existential anxieties and dilemmas very seriously and addresses itself directly to them: the need to be loved, the fear that one is thought worthless; the love of life and the fear of death. Further, the fairy tale offers solutions in ways that the child can grasp at his level of understanding (p. 10).

The decision to script these tales in verse was an easy one. Students generally have limited experience with verse, rhythm, or rhyme beyond the early years. In a sense, they are too often denied the joy of hearing and producing verse with interesting rhythmic twists and turns. Immersion in verse can entice at least some students to take risks in creating their own inventions. They may even find that they succeed where they may not have demonstrated particular competence in other genres.

Finally, it is our belief that these scripts are excellent for expanding the limited reading menus for older struggling, or ESL readers. Verse, the most memorable of all genre, has the potential to lift and carry fledgling readers over potentially rocky spots that typically would mire them down and leave them discouraged. The discovery of verse, and engagement in the genre through Readers Theatre holds promise and surprise for all students. What's more, we know that it holds rich potential to generate enthusiasm and success.

Readability

The scripts are made to be used for nearly all readers and will find excellent audience among students with varying reading abilities. The difficulty levels of the scripts are not meant for any age in particular and have utility over a span of years, around grades three to seven. It is very likely that there will be readers in grade three whose reading competency equals that of some seventh graders, and also the reverse will be true in some cases. More significantly, it is the kind of support that is offered for struggling readers to succeed even with difficult text, and the challenges that are posed for more competent readers reading relatively "easy" text, that creates a context in which all can meet to enjoy and learn in an interactive, collaborative environment.

We always invite students and teachers to begin with the oral, return to the oral, and put the spot light on the oral for special reflection. Once students become engaged in writing scripts, return to the oral as often as necessary will enable them to "listen to their writing." The developing awareness of voice, and the relationship between sound and sense, create enduring foundations for the emergence of language control in speaking, reading, and writing. This applies to work with struggling readers and ESL students even more than with students who have fewer problems learning. Wells (1988) underlines this central role of listening to language:

> The quality of children's experience as listeners to other people's stories and the richness of their own storying in dramatic play are a major influence on the ease with which they learn to make sense of print and on the quality of the stories they compose themselves. Those who have heard how written stories sound are quicker to recognize these characteristic uses of language when they meet them in the books they read and gain control of them more readily in their own writing (p. 13).

We have deliberately woven idiomatic expressions into the tales presented in this book, in part, to make some of this language accessible to struggling language users and ESL students. Further, we have not watered down the vocabulary in composing the scripts. The context, the rhythm, and the support of more competent language users should be enough to make these scripts both accessible and fun.

LEARNING AND INSTRUCTIONAL POTENTIAL

One of the special things about engagement in Readers Theatre is that you can expect the unexpected. We have found this particularly with fledgling readers who practice a script first with peers or with the support of an audio tape and offer remarks such as, " I didn't think I could read like that!" They usually read more fluently and more expressively than they thought they ever could. Once students discover that their voice is capable of getting the undivided attention of peers, they experience the joy and pride that comes from their success.

Instructional Differentiation to Meet Diverse Needs

The ultimate success of Readers Theatre comes when all are able to achieve comfortable group membership. What is particularly important is that struggling readers (and ESL students) are not perceived as second class, but as students with full membership. It also becomes important that all are encouraged to assume responsibility and ownership, sometimes even at some risk.

In the matter of engaging readers over a range of competencies and background experiences, instruction must always aim at enabling students to use sustainable strategies that characterize the independent learner. Keen observation of students will point to occasions for large group work, small group instruction, and on occasion, individual mentoring. It is important to accept the reality that just as students differ in their competencies, they will vary in what they achieve through the learning of a common text. It should not come as a surprise that some of the less able readers may "shine" quickly and unexpectedly, especially as they participate in a piece that holds special interest to them. How much mentoring and modelling has preceded, or how much support is offered during their reading doesn't matter as much as the fact that they are engaged in text, and find pleasure in the reading experience. These occasions provide a window to the expanding competence of these children, but also provide an opportunity for them to demonstrate to themselves and to the class that they have roles in the classroom community as legitimate contributing members.

How can you make full group membership in Readers Theatre a reality through instructional differentiation? Here are a few examples:

- Suppose that a piece is scripted for five readers and involves two highly competent readers, two average readers, and one reader with limited apparent competence. What is important is that we provide suggestions for a range of accommodations to enable students to achieve what they (and their teachers and parents) would have assumed "beyond reach." Sometimes it is useful to provide a less able reader with short preparatory support. You might engage the student in a "read along," or in an "echo read," or you can provide an occasion for the reader to hear another group perform the piece in order to gain familiarity with the context but also to catch the rhythm as a kind of ready scaffolding.

- Another option is to have the reader take a role in a group and double up with a stronger reader. A role performed as a duet is as legitimate as a solo read, and every bit as interesting. We have found that with inexperienced readers, a student mentor can even help by sweeping her finger underneath the text to help the struggling reader follow more easily. We do not recommend the use of highlighting role designations, but rather encourage students to always follow the text closely even as other students read.

Once the reader gains some measure of success, he/she might be provided with an unobtrusive "shadow reader" who supports the reader at his/her request, or when obvious faltering happens. We always emphasize that interesting rhythm and expressive reading take precedence over word perfect reading.

- Another alternative is to provide the reader with a taped version of the script to allow him/her to gain initial familiarity, and to use later for further support and reflection. While students should be encouraged to relinquish dependence on this kind of support as soon as possible, they should not be discouraged from re-visiting these supports, either as they take on more demanding roles, or when their confidence falters.

- So, what about the more competent, experienced readers? The biggest fear of many is that these students will be held back if they participate in a Readers Theatre with less able readers. That is a myth. There will be many occasions for these students to act as "buddies" or as short-term mentors. But also, these students can be given the opportunity to tape the scripts for use by other students. These support scripts are used for struggling readers. We suggest, however, that these tapes be monitored by teachers. Requesting an audition will suggest to students that competent reading goes far beyond mouthing the words on the page, which is a useful exercise in becoming increasingly self-reflective. It should encourage these students to appreciate the subtleties of cadence and nuance, and to the place of rhythm as they become more fluent and generally more interested readers.

- Finally, interest in differentiation connotes widening the window of "what counts" in learning and instruction. For example, so-called less able readers may often excel in their ability to be expressive, to reflect nuances that may be missed by other readers who are deemed more competent. Further, once some of the less able readers have overcome confidence issues and/or "word reading" obstacles, they may well demonstrate phrasing abilities, a sense of cadence and use of voice in reflecting irony, sarcasm, and so on, that are not necessarily apparent in some of the so-called competent readers. Even using the voice effectively to depict subtle humour demands reflective listening, and competence far beyond word reading. These are indicators of language comprehension we so often disregard or ignore. These are, however, among the language competencies that have strong potential, not only in the move to become more powerful readers, but also to inform writing processes.

Fostering Experimentation with Language

An environment in which a teacher invites students to experiment with the script and one where the teacher joins students in experimenting with different styles and nuances is likely to produce results far beyond expectations. Teachers sometimes have to release themselves from the boundaries set out in the prescribed outcomes and reach beyond to help students achieve greater things. Perhaps more than anything, it's a matter of a teacher's ability to imagine beyond what they normally see or notice in students' learning. An environment, where the imagination rules, will always open doors to student inventions that typically don't find places in the prescribed goals in the curriculum. We subscribe fully to the decades-old statement of Carl Rogers: "… if I trust the capacity of the human individual for developing his own potentiality, then I can provide him with many opportunities and permit him to choose his own way and his own direction in his own learning." (Rogers, 1969, p. 114) Engaging students in Readers Theatre is an excellent way for both students and teachers to experience the unexpected. They can achieve beyond the confines of imagination, to choose their individual direction in learning, and to trust in their choices.

The degree to which students see Readers Theatre as an occasion to take risks, and experiment with language, depends on at least three main factors:

1. **Availability of interesting scripts with twists and surprises:** Since many students have limited experience with reading poetry, rhythm, and rhyme, introduce them to some more interesting scripts. This will create the potential for a spark and more enjoyment when they read. Interesting rhythm extends the range of what is possible with the voice.

2. **Flexibility and joint ownership:** The more students are invited to make suggestions about their scripts, the more interested they will be in the process. Some suggestions for student involvement include:

   - Try varying ways of expressing the verse.
   - Change roles from solo to small group (chorus) and vice versa.
   - Add bits of costuming, sound effects, and so on.
   - Encourage students to insert more interesting words and exclamations in the scripts they read.

   The more these are encouraged the more students are likely to look for ways to enhance their productions and to render the stories more meaningful. An environment that values surprise and creativity will likely motivate students to be more creative and invested in the process.

3. **Modelling experimentation:** Students gain much when their teachers become actively involved in Readers Theatre productions. Teachers may even take on a role in the script or may act as a mentor to a reader who needs support. One of the best compliments afforded teachers is to have students invite them into partnership. This often leads to excellent brainstorming sessions in the class. Ideas emerge from questions such as, "What if we try …?" or "Let's try to introduce more direct speech from the 'big bad wolf' to compliment the reader's narration about the wolf." or "How about changing this part from solo to full chorus to give more emphasis?" There is a marked difference between the exhortation, "I want you to try …" and the milder form, "Should we try …?" Being part of the production helps students and teachers form a strong partnership. It helps create a climate to experiment where students can stretch their boundaries with minimum social risk. Griffin (2001) suggests that encouragement to engage in verbal play in a shared context has the potential to deepen the capacity both to question and to create.

Promoting Fluency in Reading (and Oral Language): Especially for ESL and Struggling Learners

Partly as a function of increased motivation to practice, and partly as a consequence of opportunities to listen to others reading fluently, participating in Readers Theatre enhances the student's ability to read. This is especially true if the Readers Theatre texts are interesting and well-formed scripts. The rhythm and rhyme acts as a kind of "auxiliary engine" that helps mobilize language, and keeps it moving forward with few speed bumps. The fact that verse is more memorable than text in prose format enables readers (and listeners) to develop a store of "language echoes" in their heads. Even less fluent readers soon discover that they are able to move forward with greater ease than they had with previous texts. Further, just being surrounded by the "buzz" of fluent reading is enabling for students. We know that singers in a choir sing more fluently than they do when they sing a solo. That is certainly the case with young and novice singers. The same is true for young readers in a Readers Theatre production.

There is potential reciprocity between the listening/reading engagement and the development of more fluent oral language "strings" or phrases. This is true more with the use of rhythmic scripts than it is for other types of texts. ESL students, unfortunately, are sometimes denied access to Readers Theatre. That is a mistake even when scripts feature words not within ESL students' vocabularies. The overall context and the rhythm allow these students to learn texts that are quite often considered too difficult for them. Further, their involvement in a Readers Theatre group is often one of the best opportunities for them to become active, contributing members of a learning community. Readers Theatre is a fun way for ESL students to showcase their learning, and express themselves creatively, as was the case with Milek, a grade five student from Poland. He was very quiet and shy in his Canadian classroom. Following a Readers Theatre performance his peers exclaimed, "We didn't know Milek could speak!" They were all very excited for Milek, and it gave him a chance to feel he belonged in the class.

Consistency, and sometimes inconsistency, occurs in the way we feel rhythms in scripts. Students, at times, become frustrated when the rhythm of a passage works well for them one day, and then the next day, they have to struggle to get the beat. This may happen simply as a result of inconsistency in placing strong beats on particular words in a script. This should not create undue stress, but rather be seen as natural. When students begin to see this as a problem, encourage them to simply try to say varying rhythms of the first few lines until they feel a satisfying beat, or encourage one of the more consistent readers to lead off with the first reader role to set the tone.

Writing Scripts

Involvement in Readers Theatre often leads students to see scripting potential in the pieces that they have written in many classes such as language arts, science, or social studies. Students may also see potential for scripts in the writing of others. Perhaps they have read a chapter in a novel and they see a natural script emerge from that author's words. Some examples of stories that make good scripts include: Chapter 12 from E.B. White's *Charlotte's Web*, or any chapter from Smucker's *Jacob's Little Giant*. Having students write scripts is an excellent way to encourage them to listen to themselves as writers. Fitch (2005) emphasizes the extent to which her writing involves listening as she explores possibilities with words. Exploring scripting possibilities enables students to become knowledgeable about the nature of text. Writing, revising, and editing scripts can highlight listening as central to the writing process, and of course, listening is central to oral production of scripts. This process of transfer will not be automatic for all students. However, we know that with some instructional nudging and demonstration, Readers Theatre, perhaps more than any other medium, presents the context for reciprocal language processes to become transparent.

Building Confidence through Experience and Success Attribution

"Apart from the optimism often engendered by a new setting and new experiences, engaging in an activity such as Readers Theatre has the potential to disclose surprises about children's competencies that they haven't been able to reveal in other more constrained settings." (Braun, 1993, p. 162) Such an experience can open the door for students to see hope, at least in part, because they begin to see a broader sweep of what's important. Some of those success markers, perceived or real, may have constrained their learning in the past. Student self-awareness will be enhanced as we initiate discussions by asking questions such as, "What was it that opened the door for you?" "What do you attribute your success to?" This self-reflection is necessary in order for students to be able to replicate their success in the future. It is doubly useful if students are able to attribute success to what they did, rather than attribute everything about the success to simple luck, or something external to themselves. This is not to say all the students' success comes from within. External factors (the prompting of a buddy, for example) also play a role. Both are important, but an over-emphasis on attributions of the external places improvement and success outside of personal control of the student, and risks the perpetuation of undue dependence on others as perceived contributors to success and failure, or even the primary source.

We believe that personal reflection on attribution, and reflective conversations with peers and the teacher enable students to re-think their identity as learners. Further, many struggling readers and writers suffer less from lack of ability than they do from self-defacing views of themselves as learners. Many of these views are a consequence of their reliance on external attributions, and a failure to monitor their own learning. Johnston (2005) believes that for resilient learners, ability is less relevant than engagement and challenge, and that they don't see their value as a person as being conditional upon ability. The more brittle learners, on the other hand, are prone to interpret difficulty with a literate task as a demonstration of lack of ability that is permanent, and as a result they systematically avoid challenging tasks (p. 685). We have long known that feelings steeped in identity, especially negative feelings, are highly resistant to change. We think that the collaborative nature of Readers Theatre, with the many opportunities for open feedback to reading and writing, allows for rare opportunities to create invitations to see hope and stretch students' visions of their competence (Braun, 2005).

Working Together in Community

Engagement in Readers Theatre allows students to come together as a community of cooperative readers. Students must work together to perfect the script and their presentation of it. Participating in Readers Theatre demands that students listen to themselves and listen to each other in order to create a successful performance. They begin to see that success can only happen through productive discussion of what needs to be done to improve and what they are already doing well. They learn negotiating skills and how to respect one another's opinions. Successful engagement in Readers Theatre depends on interpersonal relationships, but it also has strong potential for enhancing these relationships. Griffin (2001) puts it so well: "With a strategizing partner at their side and a meaningful text they [guide] each other in powerful ways." (p. 376)

Celebrating Success

We all look forward to celebrating our success. Most students are challenged to do their best when they look forward to opportunities to perform. They often find affirmation for their efforts in the reaction they receive from their audience.

Arthur, for example, was a struggling reader in the seventh grade. He attended intervention sessions at the University of Calgary Reading/Language Clinic. Initially, the student clinician worked with him on his own to help him improve his reading. As Arthur's reading progressed, he was incorporated into group sessions with other students. It was at this point that Arthur started to participate in short Readers Theatre productions within the clinic. This enabled him to emerge from his cocoon of silence and passive compliance. When it was decided to "showcase" the students for parents and teachers, a number of Readers Theatres pieces were included. Since Arthur was considerably older than the rest of the students, there was great debate about the wisdom of having him share the stage with a group of much younger children. Finally, he was given the choice. He decided that he wanted to participate, and was very successful!

In the follow-up interview five years later, when Arthur was asked to comment on highlights of his involvement in the clinical program, he responded, "Being part of the Readers Theatre at the parent and teacher program. That was the first time anyone ever applauded for me."

Arthur's reaction is typical of readers who have previously struggled and then felt empowered by success in a Reader Theatre performance. The anticipation of affirmation from an audience and the opportunity to showcase their best effort is an incentive for students to work harder. They focus more intently, and practice until they are satisfied that they have attained their best. The reaction from the audience is cause for them to be proud and to celebrate their success.

Experiencing New Beginnings

Readers Theatre is for everyone. In our experience working with students in classrooms, teachers sometimes warn us about students who will not be able to participate because of their low "reading levels." Those teachers are often skeptical when we insist on including all the students in the production. We strongly feel that the struggling readers are the ones who benefit the most from participating.

Readers Theatre is sufficiently different from those other classroom activities that have left students with fear and feelings of failure. Participating may in fact allow the struggling readers to begin to believe in the promise of success and new beginnings. To have their successes recognized and applauded by peers, teacher, and parents goes a long way in creating sustained efforts to reach higher, and into unexplored territory. New beginnings carry a promise of redefining the social lines that so often distinguish the stars and pariahs of the classroom. Repeated failure only stunts or even completely shuts down learning; glimmers of success, on the other hand, are rays of sunlight that bring hope that encourages and sustains students.

The Assessment Connection: New Observational Insights into Student Competence

Every time we add something to the curriculum spectrum, especially something interesting, we extend the range of learning we should anticipate. We are likely to see things that surprise us, and often from those students we least expect to surprise us. As students take on new roles, at least four important changes occur:

- The teacher's idea of what counts or what is important in student learning will change.
- Teachers will change their perceptions and increase expectations of struggling students and their abilities, not only in Readers Theatre, but also in other competencies.
- Students will be empowered to rethink and turn around self-perception and self-expectation.
- Readers Theatre has the potential to encourage students in the classroom community to reassess who are the "stars."

Enjoy the scripts!

References

Braun, C. *Listening, Looking and Learning: Observing and Assessing Young Readers.* Winnipeg, MB: Portage & Main Press, 1993.

Braun, C. "Dancing Beyond the Cyclone of Fads and Edicts: Children and Teachers Together." *Early Childhood Education*, 6, 3, p. 3–15, Edmonton, AB: Alberta Teachers Association, 2005

Eisner E.W. "The Kinds of Schools We Need" *Phi Delta Kappan*, 83, 8, April, p. 576–594, 2002

Fitch, S. Interview with Kathryn Gretzinger, CBC "Sounds Like Canada," June 6, 2005

Griffin, M.L. "Social Contexts of Beginning Reading" *Language Arts*, March Issue, p. 376 – 382, 2001.

P. D. Johnston. "Literacy Assessment and the Future," *The Reading Teacher*, 58, 7, April, 2005, p. 684–686, 2005.

C. Rogers. *Freedom to Learn*, Columbus, OH: Charles E. Merrill, 1969.

Little Urban Riding Girl

Adapted from a story by Reece Bennett, Grade 6
Matheson Island School
Frontier School Division, Manitoba

(For **Six Readers**)

READER 1:

Just on the edge of the city lived a girl with her Mom and Dad;
Both parents worked hard and long to pay the rent for their pad.

READER 2:

Father was a competent chef; Mother sold beautiful flowers;
Granny lived on the 32nd floor in one of the apartment towers.

READER 3:

Granny had bought a bike for her precious little "pearl"
And ever since had called her, my "Little Urban Riding Girl."

READER 1:

One day Mother told her Riding Girl that Granny had fallen ill;
She'd tried steam baths and wonder oils and just about every pill.

MOTHER:

I've packed a basket for your Granny—sandwiches and her favourite soup;
I hope that this will settle the poor old lady's croup.

READER 2:

So Riding Girl was off in a jiff, not at all worried about city dangers;
But, nearing Granny's apartment block encountered unusual strangers.

READER 3:

An unkindness of ravens, obviously famished, blocked the girl's path on the street;
And intuition suggested immediately that her basket held something to eat.

READER 1:

Little Urban Riding Girl, well-mannered in every way,
Greeted the ravenous ravens with a shaky, but kind **"Good Day!"**

RAVEN:

You seem to be rushing, little girl; what are your plans today?

LITTLE URBAN RIDING GIRL:

I'm off to see my Granny who's down with a miserable fever;
I hope that my sandwiches and soup will serve to finally relieve her.

RAVEN:

Sandwiches and soup—a banquet for birds of my kind;
For the past two months all we've had are any dry worms we could find.

READER 2:

The raven conversed with the Urban Girl till they came to the city address;
The girl was completely ignorant of doom or impending stress.

LITTLE URBAN RIDING GIRL:

I must be going, Granny is waiting in this lonely apartment block;

RAVEN:

Could I entice you to a race as I leave the rest of the flock?

READER 3:

To the girl this seemed like an innocent chat; even gave her granny's address;
The raven had proposed a curious dare, to challenge to race her, no less!

RAVEN:

> You take the stairs as fast as you can, I'll ride up in the elevator;
> Who gets their first will wait at the door; let's go for it, see you later!

READER 1:

> Quite naïve to think that she'd win, the girl was obviously taken;
> Read on to find out just how and if she'll be able to save her bacon.

READER 2:

> The raven quickly tapped on the door—faked a girlish, *"Hi, it's me;"*
> Granny called in her sweetest voice;

READER 3 (Granny):

> Do come in. I can't wait to see.

READER 1:

> Deathly afraid of ravens, Granny's voice spiked in huge crescendo;
> She dashed for the bathroom—on her way, shut off the Nintendo™.

READER 2:

> If you're aware of Red Riding Hood, whose story, no doubt, you've heard;
> I'm sure you can guess where Urban Girl will find the conniving city bird.

READER 3:

> So after, the **"knock, knock, knock,"** and the syrupy **"come in"** routine,
> We're in for another, **"how small, how large!"**
> But this is the worst I've ever seen!

LITTLE URBAN RIDING GIRL:

> Hello Granny, I've come to bring some goodies for you to eat;
> What a pathetic sight you are, though your voice still seems so sweet.

RAVEN:

> You're a bit whiny today, I'd say; it's sweet of you to come;
> I can tell you've brought some goodies, I'm famished, ain't had a crumb!

LITTLE URBAN RIDING GIRL:

> Oh, Grandma, I'm scared; you've changed; your head's ridiculously small,
> The last time I saw you, you looked so plump and tall.

RAVEN:

> My nightcap may be somewhat loose, I've come down with this rare condition;
> My head is shrivelled, and that is that, and now, please stop your fishin'.

LITTLE URBAN RIDING GIRL:
    But grandma, your eyes, so black and beady,
    And your mouth so hard and pointy. . .

RAVEN:
    My mouth may be hard and pointy—
    The better to gorge on sandwiches and soup,
    Take a hike now, child—do you get the scoop?

READER 1:
    With a piercing scream and a swoop the raven lit on the lunch;
    Pigging out on soup and sandwiches—from dried worms to this delicious brunch.

READER 2:
    But wait! This Little Urban Rider was wise beyond her years;
    Her cell phone had saved her in scrapes before, and again allayed her fears.

READER 3:
    She called her father who happened to be about;
    And in no time at all Daughter safe, and granny out!

READER 1:
    The raven, scared out of his wits by all the commotion,
    Flew the coop in a frenzied, fluttering motion.

READER 2:
    Granny sent her Little Urban Girl for sandwiches—peanut butter and jelly—
    Right near the corner of Portage and Main at a small local deli.

READERS 1, 2 & 3:
    The raven was never seen again; Granny got over her aches;
    Little Urban Riding Girl, in true tradition, preferred to bring cakes.

Little Urban Riding Girl

Out-Foxing the Big Bad Wolf

A retelling of Little Red Riding Hood

(For **Five Readers**)

READER 1:

> Long before three pigs left home to build houses of straw and wood;
> There was a girl dressed in raspberry red—her name, Little Red Riding Hood.

READER 2:

> Her Mom packed a basket to take to granny who'd called that she was sick;
> The flu, a chill, or was it gout? or heartburn? Have your pick.

READER 1:

> Covered in a hood of brilliant red, the little girl hurried on;
> Aware that she should make it there before the setting sun.

READER 2:

> She stopped to listen to the birds, picked flowers along the way;
> Never noticed anything till—she heard this gruff,

WOLF: **Good day!**

READER 1:

> The child was not at all distressed
> By this unexpected greeting;
> Promptly curtsied and replied
> With the sweetest, cheery greeting.

RED RIDING HOOD:

> Good day to you, my furry friend,
> We haven't met before;
> I'm loaded down with goodies
> To leave at Granny's door.

WOLF:

> How nice of you to think of her,
> So brave, so very kind.
> How do you get to Granny's house?
> Please, if you don't mind.

RED RIDING HOOD:

I'm taking the shortest forest route to Granny's north side dwelling.
It's cream with a bit of brownish trim; **OOPS!** Mom warned against my telling![1]

READER 2:

Red Riding Hood had done it now, but still no thought of danger;
But, she had disclosed her destination to an unknown toothy stranger.

READER 1:

The wolf's eyes sparkled with an evil glint, as he left her on the walk.
He turned his gaze toward Granny's house, his heart, as hard as rock.

READER 2:

The girl skipped happily along the mossy forest floor,
Quite confident about the route, she'd made the trek before.

READER 1:

Back to the wolf, who by this time is knocking with "all four;"
Pleading with dear old Granny to unlatch the blessed door!

GRANNY:

Who's knocking at my door? I'm suffering from the shakes!

WOLF:

It's just Red Riding Hood, I've come to bring some cakes.

GRANNY:

How awfully sweet of you to come,
Just lift the bobbin, dear.
I'll keep the shakes just to myself,
There's nothing here, to fear.

READER 2:

Poor old Granny was forced
Into a closet used for wood.
Into bed with cap and gown,
Wolf waited for Miss Hood.

READER 1:

You've guessed what happened
After that—a gentle, timid tap;
Wolf responded from his bed,
Drool dripping on his lap.

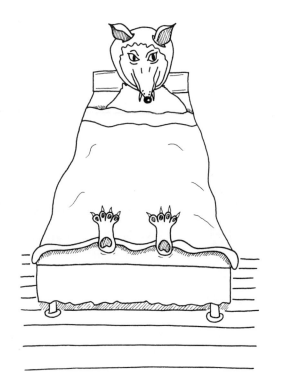

Out-Foxing the Big Bad Wolf

[1] Reader note: This is an aside to the audience, not spoken directly to the wolf.

WOLF:
> Who's calling at this hour? I'm stuck on my old couch;
> Pull the bobbin, and do come in, I'm very ill, I vouch.

READER 2:
> The fiendish wolf, with toothish grin, faked a grannyish kind of smile;
> Reluctantly, the girl approached, although it took awhile.

WOLF:
> Come here, my Riding Hood, the better to see you, my child.

READER 3:
> Little by little, the girl moved on toward this monster from the wild.

RED RIDING HOOD:
> Your eyes don't look like Granny's eyes, there's something very strange.
> I've never known an illness to bring about such change.

READER 1:
> The little girl inched on in fear, not sure what she should do.
> Visions of Dead Riding Hood, what to do, **BOO HOO!**

RED RIDING HOOD:
> Those gargantuan ears, dear Granny, am I seeing right?
> I think I saw them in the woods, I'm beginning to see the light.

READER 2:
> The girl continued with the natter, her soft voice, by now shaking.

RED RIDING HOOD:
> Are you really my old Granny? Or is this wolfish faking?

WOLF:
> Come closer, child, and take my hand, I know you love your Granny.

READER 1:
> She noticed fur on Granny's hand; how utterly uncanny!

READER 2:
> And then that terrible row of choppers gleamed in the lowering sun;
> There was no question at this point, Miss Hood had better run!

READER 1:

With light'ning speed the wicked wolf pursued the frenzied child;
But lucky for her, a woodsman had noticed them in the wild.

READER 2:

He hastened to the rescue without the least delay.
With single mind, he pulled the bobbin, and made that animal pay.

READER 1:

The chase about to follow, a most hilarious sight!
The nightgown caught the doorknob to Granny's keen delight.

READER 2:

The wolf was never seen again, granny forgot her shakes;
The last we know about this tale, the three sat down for cakes.

Out-Foxing the Big Bad Wolf

Cleverness, Cunning, and a Wolf Sent Running

A retelling of Lon Po Po—A Chinese Tale
(For **Seven Readers**)

READER 1:
>Three daughters left to their own devices, as Mama pays a visit to granny,
>A basket of goodies, mama's farewell, a lurking wolf, how uncanny.

MAMA:
>Latch the door, my dears; and don't let strangers in,
>Sleep tight, don't let the bedbugs bite, I'll see you in the mornin'.

READER 2:
>No sooner had mama gone, the wolf, up to his tricks,
>No huff or puff as in that German tale where he trashed a house of sticks.

READER 3:
>He rushed at the door and knocked with a pounding and clatter;
>The children worried—no doubt that something was the matter.

READERS 1, 2 & 3 (Children):
>Who is it? Who is it?

READER 4:
>The three children implored, a little apprehensive
>About who might be outside the door.

WOLF:
>It's your granny, your Po Po,

READER 3:
>Came the scritchy-scratchy reply.

LI HUA:
>Our mother is on her way to your place;

READER 2:
>Li Hua stated, not catching the lie.

WOLF:
Not at all strange we didn't meet, I took the round-about loop;
So just pull the latch and let me in, now that you've got the scoop.

READER 2:
Li Hua, the eldest, wasn't so sure, of the voice beyond the door.

LI HUA:
Why does your voice scritch and scratch, Po Po, whom we all adore?

WOLF:
I've caught a chill, cold air is making me worse;
Let your Po Po in for a rest,

READER 3:
Snarled the wolf, in words, by now terse.

READER 4:
Chaoxing and Tao Tao, happy as clams, to think their Po Po had come to visit,
Flew to the door and shouted,

READERS 1 & 2 (Chaoxing & Tao Tao):
Po Po, our favourite!

READER 3:
Without missing a beat, the wolf blew out the candle.
The children were suddenly scared, this was more than they could handle.

READER 4:
The two youngest clung to Po Po, wanting to be cuddled,
Li Hua had her suspicions, her thoughts now quite befuddled.

READER 1:
The old wolf soon feigned sleepiness, and climbed into the big, pillowy bed.

READER 2:
Li Hua and Tao Tao snuggled in on one side,

READER 3:
Chaoxing nestled close to the wolf's head.

READER 4:
Li Hua brushed against the bushy tail, and uttered in dismay,

LI HUA:

Po Po, your foot is shaggy; how did it get this way?

WOLF:

Your Po Po has gathered string, lots and lots of it,
So you may weave a basket—something useful and exquisite.

READER 3:

Li Hua touched the old wolf's sharp claws, and recoiled in dreaded shock;

LI HUA:

Po Po, your hand is covered in thorns.

WOLF:

Oh, poppycock!

READER 2:

And he went on to explain—

WOLF:

It's Po Po's precious awl, to make shoes for each one of you,
We're sure to have a ball!

READER 1:

Li Hua, suspicious to the end, lit the candle and caught sight
Of a hairy, scary wolfish face; but again, out went the light.

READER 4:

Putting two and two together, she needed a plan so clever
To trick the wolf and save her sisters—seemed it was now or never.

LI HUA:

Dear old Po Po, would you like to eat?
Perhaps gingko nuts would be a tasty treat.

WOLF:

Po Po is quite famished, that is true,
But what is gingko, Po Po might like two.

LI HUA:

Gingko is succulent and fresh, on the tree outside the door;
You need only eat one plump fruit and you'll live forevermore.

WOLF:

Po Po is old and frail, brittle bones and stiff old knees;
Gingko nuts sound scrumptious—but it's hard to climb those trees.

READER 1:

Li Hua insisted on climbing, with her sisters, high in the tree;
And feeling safe from the beastly threat, disclosed "Po Po's" true identity.

READER 4:

Lips smacking in anticipation, the wolf waited for the three to descend;
He sat beneath the tree, his apparent lack of savvy, hard to comprehend.

READER 2:

The wolf grew impatient and finally blurted out;

WOLF:

Precious children, what are you about?

LI HUA:

Po Po, we are eating gingko nuts we've found plenty in this tree;

WOLF:

How grand, how special—now throw some down to me.

LI HUA:

You must pick gingko nuts yourself, if the magic is to work;
Po Po, we'll help you get up here, it's a task we will not shirk.

READER 3:

The girl convinced the wolf,
That this was his only hope,
And she directed him
To find a basket and a rope.

READER 4:

The gleeful wolf obeyed
Like a well-trained puppy would,
And dragged the basket
And the rope as fast as ever he could.

Cleverness, Cunning, and a Wolf Sent Running

READER 2:

> He tossed one end of the rope to Li Hua, climbed into the basket to wait,
> Li Hua pulled and pulled, but soon let her strength deteriorate.

READER 1:

> The wolf tumbled to the ground, surprised by this twist of fate,
> But Chaoxing offered to lend a hand, to offset the wolf's weight.

READER 3:

> The wolf was so obsessed with the thought of the delicious gingko,
> And impending immortality, yelled out,

WOLF:

> Heigh-ho! Let's go!

READER 1:

> The two girls yanked the basket for all they were worth;
> The rope slipped, and the wolf plummetted to earth.

READER 2:

> Through his pain and discomfort,
> The wolf snarled and wailed;
> The sisters claimed they'd lost their grip,
> And had no wish to see him impaled.

READER 3:

> The wolf still had no idea
> His soul now hung by a thread,
> His only thoughts, of the magic gingko,
> And his long life ahead.

READER 4:

> Tao Tao, the youngest of the three,
> Offered to join the throng,
> Appeasing the wolf with the idea
> That "together" they could be strong.

READER 3:

> The children tugged and tugged,
> The wolf rose higher and higher,
> Now eye to eye with a gingko nut,
> Not a clue what was about to transpire.

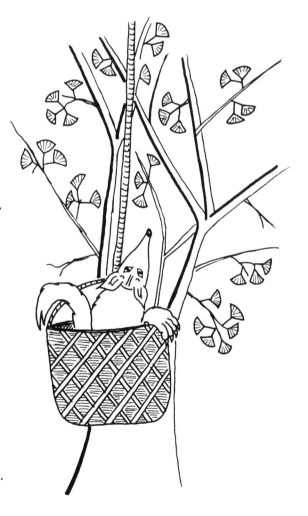

READER 2:

> The rope was released, the basket crashed down,
> The wolf came tumbling after, and like Jack, he broke his crown.

READER 1:

> The girls slowing descended from the safety of the tree,
> Checked on the wolf's condition, to make sure they were truly free.

READER 2:

> They scrambled into the house, and quickly locked the door,
> Found their way to bed, quite certain they were safe once more.

READER 3:

> When the new day dawned, their mother soon arrived,
> Laden with gifts from Po Po, so no one would be deprived.

READER 3:

> When the children told their tale of the wolf's dastardly invasion,
> Their mother was so relieved by Li Hua's power of persuasion.

READER 4:

> And that's the end of this tale—except for the scrumptious tea,
> That Po Po had provided for Mama and the three.

A Huff and a Puff—Real Scary Stuff

A retelling of The Three Pigs
- An English Tale -
(For **Six Readers**)

READER 1:

    Three little pigs, one sunny day went off without their mother.
    Old enough to think that they'd survive without each other.

READER 2:

    The first little pig, without delay, sadly left his kin.
    Unaware that very soon he'd rattle in his skin.

READER 3:

    He met a man with a load of straw
    And pleaded for a share;
    The man took pity on the hog,
    Gave all he had to spare.

READER 4:

    The pig looked for a cozy spot
    And built a little shack.
    And in no time at all
    He started to unpack.

READER 5:

    No sooner had he settled in, he thought he heard a knock;
    And with that knock, loud breathing, and the strangest wolf-like talk.

WOLF:

    Welcome to my neighbourhood, please let me in, my friend;
    Or I'll resort to huffing, and that will be your end.

READER 1 (piglet 1):

    Friend, indeed! Your threats of huffing, and your appetite for pork;
    Your reputation has long been out from Plum Coulee to New York.

READER 2:

    Poor little porker, just hadn't been around;
    Just one big huff and a little puff, a mere tail left on the ground.

READER 3:

> The second pig, no wiser than the first,
> Soon took to the road;
> Met a man with a load of sticks,
> And begged for half the load.

READER 4:

> Piglet set to work with vigour
> With his precious load of sticks;
> He rushed to finish by end of day
> Or he could be in a fix!

READER 5:

> Quite happy with his mini-mansion, he settled in with ease;
> Quite unaware of cruel eyes lurking behind the trees.

READER 3:

> Yes, indeed, the wolf had watched Piglet hard at work;
> Pork chops looming on his brain, mouth drooling! Huge, wolfy smirk.

READER 1:

> The wolf was sure that, as before, he'd out-smart the second pig;
> His powerful knock was strong enough to rattle every twig.

WOLF:

> You heard me knock on your twiggy door, this is my day for ham;
> You might as well just open up or I'll trash your door jamb.

A Huff and a Puff—Real Scary Stuff

READER 2 (Piglet 2):

I've heard of your huffing, I'm not afraid of your puffing;
I've built this house to save my stuffing.
By my chinny chin chop,
I demand that you stop.

READER 4:

A huff and a puff, and that was enough! A piglet's house in a heap!
Piglet number two—you guessed right—not an oink; not a peep!

READER 5:

Piglet three, the resourceful one,
Met a man with bricks;
A lucky find for this lonely pig;
Much better than straw or sticks.

READER 4:

He quickly set about construction,
Each brick was laid with pride;
Before one could utter, "Piggy Pork Pie,"
The jubilant pig was inside.

READER 3:

But wait! Just wait! Again, the wolf was there;
He'd dealt with straw and sticks—trashed them beyond repair.

WOLF:

A bit unfair, I should think! I've dealt with a lot of stuff;
But bricks and mortar, I'm not sure—I'm running low on Huff.

READER 2:

Piglet at the window met eyes so cold and mean;
He wondered what the wolf would try to vent his blistering spleen.

READER 1:

There was little comfort, as he watched the ravenous beast;
That the chops the wolf was licking, were not his own, at least.

READER 2:

Without a warning, not even a knock, loud puffing and thunderous kicks;
Piglet was thankful that he'd decided to construct a house of bricks.

READER 3 (Piglet 3):

Keep up your huffing and your puffing, that's what we expect of you;
Just be careful, you furry bloke, your puffer is turning blue.

READER 4:

The wolf was smarter than the average beast; a plan was up his sleeve;
And with the sweetest syrupy voice a yarn he began to weave.

WOLF:

Piglet dear, I know that you need food; if you can find a tub
I'll meet you at the market and help you find some grub.
If you will leave your house of bricks I promise to meet you sharp at six.

READER 5:

Piglet three was up at dawn;
He found his way with ease;
Made it home by five o'clock,
Loaded with carrots and peas.

READER 1:

Six o'clock sharp, and not a sign—
Of piglet here or there;
Wolf quickly went to piglet's house,
Not a moment left to spare.

WOLF:

Here I am, my little friend, you're late for our morning date;
Not to worry, we'll leave together, and enjoy our walk, dear mate.

On with your duds, my fine porker, we'll relish this morning stroll;
What I'm about to show you will keep you off the dole.

READER 3 (Piglet 3):

Pardon me for what I've done; I'm seldom really rude;
But I was up at sunrise to gather up my food.

READER 2:

The wolf was furious, hopping mad; at this four-legged hunk of bacon;
The ranting, anger and disgust left the poor beast shaken.

READER 4:

No time for pity or revenge, wolf had another thought;
He disguised his anger with aplomb, and framed a brand new plot.

A Huff and a Puff—Real Scary Stuff

WOLF:

 Dear sweet pig, please hear me out; there's an orchard up the hill;
Please meet me there at five o'clock; with buckets ready to fill.

READER 5:

The wily wolf, not to be fooled by this impudent, wicked boar;
He'd give him a dose of his medicine, and went to the orchard at four.

READER 4:

The pig was up at break of day—bought a load of apples for tea;
He spotted the wolf on top of the hill, smacking his lips with glee.

WOLF:

 I see that you're early, my succulent friend; are the apples to your taste?

READER 3:

Pig tossed an apple toward the wolf, a decision made in haste.

READER 2:

The silly old wolf pursued the fruit; piglet pleased with his fun;
Once more he had out-foxed the wolf, (If you'll excuse the pun.)

READER 1:

Poor wolf, by now, annoyed by each new blunder.
To think that this bratty little pig, again had stolen his thunder.

READER 3:

He'd try once more, and only once, to trick the cunning swine.
Once more he went to the house of bricks, to plead and coax and whine.

WOLF:

 I'm going to the country fair, you know; I'd like you to come with me.
Please meet me, you'll be glad you did; let's make it sharp at three.

READER 5:

The pig came first, and bought a churn, to make a batch of butter,
But not unnoticed by the wolf—you should have heard him mutter:

WOLF:

 I've had it with that pig; I'll get him into line;
Just one brutal wolfish charge, and it's "Goodbye, smarty swine."

READER 2:

Quick as a wink or even quicker, the pig was in the churn;
Stuffed in tight like a rolled up ham, you should have seen it turn.

READER 4:

The pig made a dash for his brick abode, things were getting tense;
He put his piggy brain in gear, to plan his next defense.

READER 1:

He poured some water in a pot, and put it on high heat;
The wolf came scrambling down the chimney; unaware of sure defeat.

READER 3:

What a tumult! What a splatter! You should have seen him dive;
Wolf hit the boiling water, no chance that he'd survive.

READER 2:

The smug, industrious porker knew his smarts were "top-flight,"
He had learned that the huff of a wolf is bigger than his bite.

READER 1,2 & 3:

And that's the tale of three young pigs, and a wolf with a cruel streak;

READERS 4 & 5:

And one ingenious pig who out-smarted the beast
In a steamy game of hide-and-seek.

A Huff and a Puff—Real Scary Stuff

Seven Kids and a Wolf on the Skids

A retelling of a Wolf and Seven Kids
(For **Five Readers and Chorus**)

READER 1:

A Nanny Goat and her seven kids lived in a ramshackle shack;
A rickety place, but some relief from worry of attack.

READER 2:

One day as she was leaving, to gather up some food;
There was no doubt that she had qualms for the safety of her brood.

MOTHER GOAT:

Listen, you kids, I shall be back; there's a wolf with eyes of steel;
One crack in the door, and you'll be served as a scrumptious seven-course meal.

KID CHORUS:

Please, trust us, mother, we'll guard with care.
We're more than wise to a wolfish dare!

Though how will we know it's you or the beast?
He'll try every trick for a mint jelly feast.

MOTHER GOAT:

His voice is gruff; mine is sweet,
Good-bye now, kids, I'm off on the beat.

READER 3:

In a matter of minutes, a gravelly voice startled the young kids' ears;
Instant confirmation of mother's dreaded fears.

WOLF:

Let me in, do let me in, I've brought you a surprise;
Please lift the latch, and I'll come in; you won't believe your eyes!

KID CHORUS:

Shame on you, you ugly creature, you can't fool us, you know!
If we open up the door you'll have us in one blow.

Our mother's voice is sweet and clear, yours is loud and gruff;
Our mother has often warned us not to fall for your wolfish bluff.

READER 1:

The wolf gave up on these smart kids, or so it seemed, at least;
Remember though, conniving once gained him a two-pig feast.

READER 2:

Of all the things that wolves will try, this one takes the cake!
He swallowed chalk in an enormous gulp, his voice now, a cunning fake.

READER 3:

He took off for the house of kids, chalk scratching his sore throat;
By this time, starved and quite annoyed; those kids had got his goat!

WOLF:

Please let me in, do let me in; I've discovered a marvelous deal;
Please open up so we can have a truly scrumptious meal.

KID CHORUS:

Our mother, indeed! Show us your feet;
We know you are desperate for a whack of kid meat.

READER 1:

The kids took one look at those coal black paws upon the window ledge;
Their taunts and their derision sent the wolf right "off the edge."

READER 2:

The wolf took off in utter rage, down to Baker's Street.
He must have used his wolfish charm to get flour on his feet.

READER 3:

In minutes, that seemed like seconds, the wolf knocked at the door;
This time with a brand new ploy, one never tried before.

Seven Kids and a Wolf on Skids

WOLF:

Please let me in, I'm very tired, I've had a long, hard day;
I've come home to eat, just open up, I pray!

KID CHORUS:

Put your feet right on the ledge, so we can tell it's you;
Had we not been cautious we'd already be goat stew.

READER 1:

The wolf, again, displayed his paws; this time they were pure white.
The kids, of course, unlocked the door, first panicked, then took flight.

READER 2:

They soon ran out of hiding spots, wolf's tongue was all alop!
He pounced upon the first poor kid in one giant belly flop.

READER 3:

The little waif was little more than the hungry wolf's hors d'oevres.
The next three, would you believe—mere appetizer serves.

READER 2:

He hunted down the next two kids—that left only one to stalk.
The smartest one of the whole kid lot hid in the grandfather clock.

READER 3:

Imagine how the old beast felt, after eating the six-pack lot;
He fell asleep in anguish, his stomach, one huge knot.

READER 1:

Poor mother entered the open door, a large lump in her throat.
She looked and looked, but quite in vain, to find a billy goat.

MOTHER GOAT:

I'm here, I'm here, where are you all? I asked you not to roam.

READER 2:

Then she spied the sleeping wolf right inside her very home.

READER 1:

A tiny voice came from the clock; it sounded like her kid.
She dashed across the room and opened up the lid.

READER 2 (Little Kid):

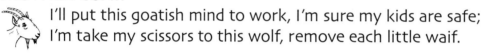 I found a place inside the clock, not so, the other six.
The big bad wolf deceived us, left us in a fix!

READER 3:

Mom took one look at the sleeping wolf, wild heaving in his belly.
The mother knew in an instant the contents wasn't jelly.

MOTHER GOAT:

I'll put this goatish mind to work, I'm sure my kids are safe;
I'm take my scissors to this wolf, remove each little waif.

READER 1:

Then she told each little kid to find a large, large stone.
Threw them pell-mell into the wolf, and stitched him to the bone.

READER 2:

The wolf awakened just before the goat had finished stitching;
He howled and moaned in terrible pain, writhing, heaving, twitching.

READER 3:

He rubbed sleep from his weary eyes, yawned and tried to stretch;
Rocks settling in the bottom now; you should have heard him wretch!

READER 1:

His great discomfort, and his thirst drove him to the water;
Feeling more hunger than he'd felt before the slaughter.

READER 2:

As the wolf was bending forward, the stones slid toward his head;
He took one giant tumble and lined the river bed.

READERS 1, 2 & 3:

That's the story of this Nanny Goat and her seven little kids;
A lesson in craft and cunning, to put a wolf on skids.

Seven Kids and a Wolf on Skids

A Prince, A Lass, and A Slipper of Glass

A retelling of Cinderella

(For Five Readers)

READER 1:

> The story's told of a special girl; her name was Cinderella;
> Her father who adored his child, was a loving sort of fella.

READER 2:

> In spite of father's special traits, he made a fateful error;
> He married a mean old witch—Cinderella's eternal terror.

READER 3:

> This woman had two lazy girls, oh, how they would connive,
> As Cinderella's name implies she struggled to survive.

READER 1:

> The elder sisters got a note; an invite to a ball.
> They fussed and fussed over gems and laces—attire to the Prince's hall.

READER 2 (Sister 1):

> I need more gems and rubies to adorn this magnificent figure;
> You're trying to out-do me, Sis; not this time, I guess, by jigger!

READER 3 (Sister 2):

> I know that I'm the fairest, my braids will be in French;
> And I know I'll get assistance from that lowly cinder wench.

CINDERELLA:

> I'll help you, though I know, that both of you are schemers;
> I'll see you safely to the coach—not much choice for dreamers.

FAIRY GODMOTHER:

Why are you crying, fair young maid? I'll share my magic schemes;
I will cast a spell on you beyond your wildest dreams.

CINDERELLA:

Oh, how I wish that I could go to the Prince's ball tonight.
It's a silly dream, I know that; it's wild, quite out of sight.

FAIRY GODMOTHER:

I'll help you out of your dilemma, a pumpkin will do the trick;
Go fetch the largest you can find, then I will do my schtick.

READER 1:

No sooner was the pumpkin scooped, a golden coach appeared;
And with that touch, so to speak, Cindy's coast was cleared.

CINDERELLA:

Let me guess, dear Godmother, a mouse trap you now desire?
You'll give each mouse a magic nudge—**VOILA!** Six white steeds will transpire!

A Prince, A Lass, and A Slipper of Glass

FAIRY GODMOTHER:

My brilliant child, you're learning fast; that's exactly what I'll do.
And brand new threads, let's not forget and sparkling new glass shoes.

Be home at midnight, and you will see the power of my magic;
A minute late, and you will find the consequences tragic.

READER 2:

MEANWHILE. . .

READER 3:

The attired sisters left for the ball that night;
Cinderella followed, gussied up, sisters barely out of sight.

READER 1:

It seemed an instant, and there she was the centre of the ball;
Exquisite beauty, just sheer charm, hushed "ahhs" throughout the hall.

READER 2:

She charmed the Prince, the King, the Queen, virtually everybody there;
Who she was, or why she'd come, nobody was aware.

READER 3:

Exactly at the quarter hour, before the stroke of midnight,
She bade adieu to everyone—a picture of sheer delight.

READER 2:

She met her sisters at the gate, endured the nitter-natter;
Cinderella just stood by and listened to the chatter.

READER 1:

Got lost in the conversation, the evening so sublime!
And then, impending doom she felt at the clang of the midnight chime.

READER 2:

She dissolved into a whirlwind; went flying through the door,
All that people could recall—a girl in rags—no more!

READER 3:

No coach, no carriage, just two fast legs, you'd think that this would flip her;
Like a doe with the wind on her back to her home with one glass slipper.

READER 1:
    The other slipper firmly clutched by the Prince taken by surprise;
    He quickly dispatched a herald to match the slipper's size.

READER 2:
    Every damsel tried the slipper, what an horrendous to-do!
    Even Cindy's homely sisters thrust foot into the shoe.

READER 3:
    And then came Cinderella's turn, though still dissolved in tears;
    Her sisters were beside themselves; cast taunts and cruel jeers.

READER 1:
    The taunting and the jeering came to a sudden halt;
    The slipper clearly matched her foot, even to a fault.

READER 2:
    Amazement, surprise, and utter joy pervaded the princely palace;
    Even the cruel sisters adjusted, with a minimum of malice.

READERS 1, 2 & 3:
    And so the story ends with a HOO! HAA! royal marriage;
    What a happy ending—complete with a pumpkin carriage.

                A Prince, A Lass, and A Slipper of Glass

A Sage, A Fish, and Yeh-Shen's Wish

A retelling of Yeh-Shen—A Chinese Tale

(For **Seven Readers**)

READER 1:

Long ago, in ancient China, lived Yeh-Shen, an orphan child,
Skin as smooth as fresh-spun silk, the image of sunshine when she smiled.

READER 2:

But, Yeh-Shen's stepmother with a heart as hard as nails;
Had harsh words and cruel jibes, clearly reminiscent of other tales.

READER 3:

Stepmom would shout orders from dawn til night;

READER 4:

Yeh-Shen was filled with dread—a victim of unrelenting spite.

READER 5:

Hard to imagine a fate so cruel, but add a stepsister named Wu Chan
Who goaded Yeh-Shen at every turn, like only a bully can.

READER 4:

There was, however, sparse respite, which she found in the courtyard pond—
Yeh-Shen and a fish with jewelled scales soon formed a special bond.

READER 2:

Yeh-Shen, half-starved, shared her meagre fare with her friend in the sparkling pool;
Quite aware that her involvement there defied the courtyard rule.

READER 3:

Stepmother was a sneaky witch and soon sensed the special bond.
She kept an evil eye focussed on "doings" around the pond.

READER 1:

But the beautiful, bejewelled fish fortunately had a clever streak,

READER 5:

And quickly engaged the witch in games of hide and seek.

READER 1:

Anger consumed the nasty woman, her trickery not yet used,
Disguised herself in Yeh-Shen's coat, headed for the pond, not at all amused.

READER 2:

The fish, seeing the tattered coat, expecting morsels from a friend,
Swam toward the pool's edge,

READER 3:

And never suspected the dasterdly end.

READER 4:

Stepmother felt no remorse as she plunged a dagger into the fish,
And thought she had cleverly disguised her deed by cooking a tasty dish.

READER 5:

As the sun set beyond the city wall, Yeh-Shen searched in vain;
No sign of her friend in the glimmering pool, unaware of her stepmom's distain.

READER 4:

She'd hardly had a chance to grieve when a voice gave her quite a scare,
She was curious when she saw an ancient soul look on her with care.

SAGE:

Your fish is gone, your stepmother guilty of the slaughter,
Hardly surprising, so jealous is she of her lovely stepdaughter.

YEH-SHEN:

I knew she didn't like me, but my stepmother, so filled with hate?

READER 3:

Yeh-Shen listened to the news and found it hard to relate.

YEH-SHEN (aside):

The fish, indeed, is dead, but there must be some mistake,
I must be wary of this old stranger, perhaps he is a fake.

A Sage, A Fish, and Yeh-Shen's Wish

SAGE:

    Your friend, the fish, is a gift; its bones charged with wonderful magic;
    Use their power when you need a lift from your life which is so tragic.

READER 2:

    Questions sprang from Yeh-Shen's mouth, but the old sage had headed south.

READER 1:

    She hid the fish bones away, speaking to them almost everyday.

READER 5:

    Yeh-Shen, careful not to waste a wish, only asked each day for a tasty dish.
    She sneaked away from stepmother's rule, who day by day became more cruel.

READER 1:

    Spring Festival was coming near,
    The most exciting time of year.

READER 2:

    Young girls hoped to snag a beau,
    An important reason to go.

READER 3:

    Yeh-Shen dreamed of a chance,
    To meet someone and share a dance.

READER 4:

    But her stepmother made sure she was banned,
    So her own daughter could offer her hand.

READER 5:

    The special day finally arrived,

READER 3:

    And just as the old witch had contrived,

READER 1:

    She and her daughter dressed in their best,
    Headed to the banquet with the rest.

READER 4:

    Sad, and all alone, Yeh-Shen spoke to the bones of her fish,

YEH-SHEN:

>To go to the festival—that's my one and only wish.
>All I have are these sad-looking rags;
>I only belong with the old hags.

READER 2:

>Then magically transformed—a gown of the finest silk draped her like a butterfly,
>Delicate slippers of gold slid onto her feet, and in her joy she began to cry.

READER 1 (Bones):

>You're ready to fly, to have a good time,
>But the slippers of gold, must be returned in this rhyme.

READER 2:

>Sang out the spirit of her friend, as Yeh-Shen whisked away,
>To join the throngs celebrating toward the closing of day.

READER 3:

>Yeh-Shen, with her swaying and swirling, made quite the showing,

READER 4:

>Attracting attention without her really knowing.

READER 5:

>How fine if this were the ending, but Stepmother and daughter were suspicious,

READER 4:

>The resemblance was uncanny; their intentions, of course, malicious.

READER 3:

>Yeh-Shen fled the scene, lost a slipper along the path,
>Returned to her former self, and now feared the fishbones' wrath.

READER 2:

>The bones were silent, the spirit inert;
>Yeh-Shen's pleading fell on the dust and the dirt.

READER 1:

>**MEANWHILE,**

READER 3:

>The tiny shoe was found and delivered with care to the King,
>Who found its beauty enchanting, and wondered who'd wear such a thing!

READER 5:
    The search was on,

READER 2 & 4:
    Over hill, over dale,

READER 3 & 5:
    Large feet, small feet, smelly feet,

ALL:
    But all to no avail!

READER 1:
    A new plan was devised—one the king would supervise;

READER 2:
    The slipper was placed in a pavilion, the rightful owner to claim the prize.

READER 3:
    Amazing how it happens that women who stand no chance
    Will force their foot into a slipper as if they'd worn it to the dance.

READER 4:
    Stepmother and daughter were hardly an exception, they each grimaced and groaned,
    As they tried on the golden shoe, exclaiming

READERS 1 & 2:
    That's the one I owned!

READER 5:
    The king was quite discouraged but persevered into the night,
    Hoping that a rare beauty would enter into his sight.

READER 3:
    Yeh-Shen had left her home when the others were asleep
    Crept into the pavilion, not daring to make a peep.

READER 1:

One quick examination convinced her it was the missing shoe;
She reached down to retrieve it and knew what she must do.

READER 4:

Taking the slippers back to the bones was really her only plan,
She was completely unaware of the hidden royal man.

READER 2:

The king, at first, was horrified, by this seemingly undeterred presumption,

READER 5:

The rags Yeh-Shen wore caused him to leap to a negative assumption.

READER 4:

The moon drifted from behind a cloud and lit Yeh-Shen's delicate face;
The king no longer noticed that she was really out of place.

READER 3:

Yeh-Shen went home to hide the slippers, no clue she'd been seen;
The impending knock on the door completely unforeseen.

READER 2:

The king and his men had followed her home,

READERS 1 & 2:

The only chance to be part of this poem.

READER 3:

And this is where we get the real Cinderella story—
Special slippers, and a girl transformed to her former glory.

READER 4:

The king overcome by her beauty, knew he had found his true love;
Yeh-Shen felt in her heart she was as free as a dove.

READER 5:

As in most tales of this vintage, they lived happily ever after;
And stepmother and daughter, banished to their cave, soon met with disaster.

A Buckskin Fella Finds Cinderella

A First Nation Tale

(For **Seven Readers**)

READER 1:
> In the land of the Wabaniki,
> Lived three orphaned sisters—
> The older two, handsome and vain,
> And a younger one, timid and plain.

READER 2:
> Working together to make their way, they were potters of some repute;
> Oochigeas, the youngest, endured ill treatment without dispute.

READER 3:
> Oona, the eldest, wove baskets from ash, and Obit used clay for the base;
> Then Oochigeas would bake the piece as the hot blast scorched her face.

READER 4:
> In time her hair was badly singed, with burns her face was marred;
> She was mocked, and named Oochigeas, rudely meaning, "One who's scarred."

READER 5:
> Glooscap, the Great Chief of the tribe knew of the mockery and spite;
> Yet wouldn't lift a finger to relieve the young girl's plight.

READER 4:
> Marten, the servant went to the chief to plead in a benevolent tone,
> The Chief advised he could only help once she could stand on her own.

READER 2:
> Now, on the far side of the lake lived Team, a young Indian man.
> He had power to become invisible and could execute just about any plan.

READER 3:
> Having this magical power relieved him of typical needs,
> Of guns, or arrows, and such things; bare hands took care of his deeds.

READER 1:

It so happened, that one day, Team's sister, excitement oozing "over the brim;"
Announced that her special brother would marry the first who could see him.

READER 2:

Though no one had ever seen him, the sister's frank dispatch
Stirred great excitement far and wide—with hunting prowess, a princely "catch."

READER 3:

Unmarried maidens flocked across the lake with zeal and joy,
Never doubting that their charm would stir the invisible boy.

READER 4:

Then, finally all that was left—three sisters, the well-known potters—
Fairy tales are often laced with strains of underdogs—especially like daughters.

READER 5:

Which one would entice this rare dude so famous far and wide?
Oona and Obit donned beautiful robes and rowed to the other side.

READER 4:

Team's sister greeted the twosome and took them to her wigwam.
Waiting for her brother's return—sisters poised to nab the "plum."

READER 3:

No paddle, no nothing, was visible as the canoe approached the shore;
The wily sisters tried every trick to become the one to score.

READER 2:

Team's sister begged the question—

SISTER:

Are you able to see him now?

READER 5:

Obit fell into the sister's trap, declared,

READER 1 (Obit):

I see him there. **OH, WOW!**

READER 5:

Oona, not to be out-done by her sister's cheap pretense,
Pretended that she, too, saw him—her only sure defense.

READER 3:

Quickly the vigilant sister knew at least one had lied;
She put them to a simple test; only one could be his bride.

SISTER:

Tell me about Team's shoulder strap?

READER 1:

The sister challenged the two; puzzled, the girls began to guess;
Clearly, neither knew.

READER 4:

To punish the wicked sisters, for failing the test of the strap;
She asked them to help with the evening meal; clearly, another trap.

READER 2:

Team was greeted by his sister, as it was time for them to eat;
The girls were warned that Team ate only at one particular seat.

READER 5:

It soon became clear to the girls that they wouldn't know his place;
Guessing and arguing would never serve them in this case.

READER 4:

Obit was asked to relieve Team of his catch of invisible meat;
Befuddled, she was unable to find it till it dropped full-force on her feet.

SISTER:

Pull Team's moccasins off his feet,

READER 3:

Became Oona's failed test case; the moccasins sailed through the air
And slapped the poor girl's face.

READER 2:

So that left Oochigeas, the sister, plain—challenged to meet this fella—
Who could tell that she might become the prima aboriginal Cinderella!

READER 5 (Team):
My bride is a long time coming.

READER 1:
Mooned Team as he heard the girls moan;

SISTER:
Patience, my brother, you want one who's truthful, not some conniving drone.

READER 2:
Oona and Obit returned to their home to vent their bitter frustration;
Oochigeas had no recourse but to escape their degradation.

READER 3:
She fled far into the woods, to reflect in a quiet, secluded spot;
Relieved her heart with bitter tears, then settled in serious thought.

READER 4:
Her sisters had failed to nab Team. Slim chance, with her face so scarred;
But then, her heart began to race;

OOCHIGEAS:
Though plain, my spirit is unmarred.

READER 5:
She gathered sheets of birchbark, and cut leggings, gown, and cap;
Sewed the bark together with blades of grass, bound together scrap upon scrap.

READER 4:
Her attire was stiff and crackled as she slowly returned to her place;
She found Obit's discarded mocassins, no false pride, no feelings of disgrace.

A Buckskin Fella Finds Cinderella

READER 3:

She announced to her wicked sisters her plans to gain Team's attention;
They guffawed, they scoffed and ridiculed;

READER 2:

Hurled insults at her insane pretension.

READER 1:

Oochigeas ran through the village stung with each insult and barb;
People laughed and rolled on the ground at her outrageous scrub woman's garb.

READER 3:

Loudly, they jeered as she rushed by, sure that each taunt would reach her—

VILLAGERS:

Why birch bark rather than skins—you unspeakably ugly creature!

READER 5:

Her heart still stung with the insults as she thought of Team's sister's reaction;

READER 2:

The call of the wood, the calm of the lake,

READER 4:

Gave relief, at the least, some distraction.

READER 5:

Oochigeas met Team's sister at the door; she plainly announced her scheme:

OOCHIGEAS:

Against my sisters' threats and pleas, I have come to check out Team.

READER 4:

Oochigeas looked pleadingly at the sister; struck with the kind attention;

READER 3:

It was obvious that the sister, too, was struck,
With this openness—no pretension.

READER 2:

Before the setting sun, upon the shore,
They communed in silence with each other.

READER 1:

The sister's question broke the stillness,

SISTER:

Are you able to see my brother?

READER 2:

Oochigeas gazed with strong intent as the light was growing dim;
Then with sinking heart she said,

OOCHIGEAS:

Oh, how I wish I could see him!

READER 4:

The sister urged her to look again;

SISTER:

Perhaps his shoulder strap will show.

READER 1:

And with the most melodious gasp;

OOCHIGEAS:

I see glorious colours of the rainbow.

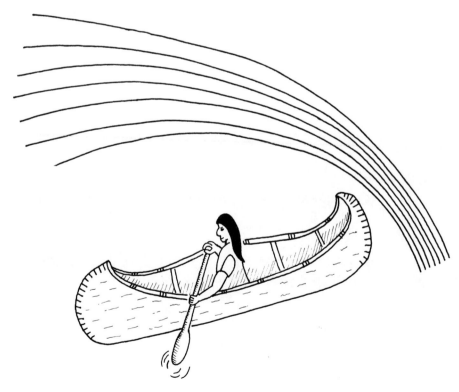

A Buckskin Fella Finds Cinderella

READER 3:

   The sister, elated at her reply introduced her brother with pride,
   She knew that before them, finally, stood his long awaited bride.

READER 4:

   She stripped the bride of her ugly clothes and tidied up her hair;
   Oochigeas looked gorgeous in doeskin, her face glowed in miraculous repair.

READER 2:

   Team was jubilant as he shouted;

READER 5 (Team):

   I have found my lovely bride.

READER 1:

   Completely overcome with awe—Oochigeas would ever be at his side.

READER 3:

   No glass slipper, not even ashes; but a princely kind of fella—
   And a maiden with all the qualities of that other Cinderella.

READERS 1 & 2 :

   And though there's no fairy godmother—there's a sister who is clever;

ALL:

   But more important than anything—two people together—happy forever.

The Snowmaiden

A Russian Tale

(For **Five Readers**)

READER 1:

A peasant woman and her husband in a strange land, far away;
One day heard the village children heartily absorbed in play.

READER 2:

They looked across at the children, then something tugged at the pair,
You see, they had no children—it seemed life had been less than fair.

READER 3:

Childless couples are not new to tales—some tempted fate with gingerbread dough,
But since that was reputed to end in disaster, this couple resorted to snow.

READERS 1, 2 & 3:

With deep longing in her heart, Svetlena sighed:

SVETLENA:

 If only we could have a wee one, to shield us when we're old;
Someone to love and adore—a gift worth a world of gold.

IVANOFF:

 Someday, who knows, our dream may come true, in the meantime, let's not fuss;
Let's go out and make a snowman, at the very least, to amuse us.

READER 1:

Indeed, this was a strange request for one who was getting old;
But no matter, in "one lamb-tail shake" the two were out in the cold.

READER 2:

Carefully they rolled, and molded and shaped, and watched the snowbeing grow;
Then to their utter surprise, the two laid eyes, not on a man, but on a maiden of snow.

READER 3:

They found blue beads for cheery eyes, a red ribbon with the brightest glow;
They stood back, and with great admiration bowed to their maiden of snow.

IVANOFF:

 Such a beautiful Snegurochka!

50

SVETLENA:

 Yes, Snegurochka! That's our beautiful snowmaiden!

READERS 1, 2 & 3 :

Something strange began to happen—both rubbed their eyes in awe,
Wondering whether they were seeing right—a slight movement of the jaw?

SVETLENA:

 Oh husband, dear husband, I'm afraid of what I'm thinking;
Those lips are forming smiling lines, and I see those eyelids blinking.

IVANOFF:

 Oh, dear one! I think this is a miracle—a miracle out of the blue!
Mark my word, indeed a smile—clearly meant for you!

READER 1 :

The astonished couple just stood there, relishing in the glow.
How could they be so lucky to have this maid of snow!

READER 2 (Snowmaiden):

I've come to be your daughter; don't be shocked, and please don't fear,
I will always care for you—you will always have me near.

READER 3 :

At last the couple had a daughter—with eyes of crystal blue,
Flaxen hair right down to her waist, almost too good to be true.

READER 1 :

When Snegurochka wasn't playing with kids she'd knead the dough for their bread,
Or stir the soup for her mother—make sure that the family was fed.

READER 2:

> Snegurochka was, from all accounts, a perfect match for the pair;
> She was helpful, kind, and caring, performed each task with flair.

READER 3:

> But, as the winter turned to spring, Snegurochka began to change;
> She avoided the outdoors completely—she was quickly seen as strange.

READERS 1, 2 & 3:

> The parents were getting worried; their daughter was shunning her friends;
> As the season grew warmer and warmer, Snegurochka soon was at loose ends.

READER 1:

> One day friends invited the snowmaiden to join them in the woodland glade;
> While the others were picking berries Snegurochka remained in the shade.

READER 2:

> In the evening the friends built a fire; they danced right over the flames;
> Snegurochka chose the icy river over the hotter campfire games.

READER 3:

> She longed to join in the laughter, the teasing, the banter, and fun;
> But something clearly held her back—perhaps, fear of coming undone.

READER 1:

> The maiden observed from the river till darkness enshrouded the troupe;
> It became harder and harder to resist the nudgings and jibes from the group.

READER 2:

> They called,

READERS 1, 2 & 3 (friends):

> Come join us, come join us, jump over the fire!

READER 3:

> Cautiously, she took one step; she would finally join in the play;
> Then dashed for the fire—took one big leap, and as quickly she melted away!

READER 1, 2 & 3:

> As for that little old man and his wife, there was no sadness, no feelings of woe;
> They would forever be blessed with memories of a maiden fashioned from snow.

The Magic Scythe

An Icelandic Tale

(For **Five Readers**)

READER 1:

> A certain workman once set out for the north to cut some hay,
> But in the mountains, storm and mist caused him to lose his way.

READER 2:

> Afraid to continue his journey, he pitched his tent and ate;
> Never thinking that the food he'd eat would turn out to work as bait.

READER 3:

> And yes, indeed, a fierce-eyed dog followed the scent to the spot,
> Devoured chunks of bread and meat—disappeared in the mist like a shot.

READER 4:

> Having finished his supper, the exhausted man slumped down in a tired heap;
> With his saddle as a pillow under his head, he soon drifted off to sleep.

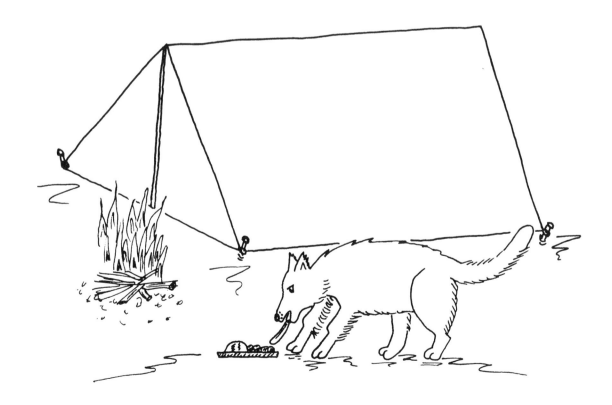

READER 1:

> In his dream, an old elf-woman softly entered his tent;
> She had a message for him, and this is how it went:

ELF-WOMAN:

> I owe you so much, dear man, for the kindness to my daughter in need;
> I have no money, but as a reward I leave you this scythe for your deed.
>
> Think well of this gift; it will prove useful to you;
> But never temper it with fire—a simple sharpening will do.

READER 2:

> And with that advice the woman left;

READER 3:

> (Remember, the man was dreaming;)

READER 4:

> In the morning, he woke up to find no mist, but a glorious sun gleaming.

READER 3:

> Quickly he gathered up his things—from food to togs to spade;
> And then picked up the saddle which had concealed a blade.

READER 4:

> A rusty scythe before his eyes, then the memory of the night;
> He quickly loaded it in his pack, and on his horse took flight.

READER 1:

> He soon discovered the road which the night mist had concealed,
> And made all speed for his destination—the northland haying field.

READER 2:

> He reached the northern country, but the haying season had passed;
> Luckily, he heard of a woman who left her haying to the last.

READER 3:

> Indeed, she had a reputation of leaving her haying undone.

READER 4:

> It could have been that she wanted the hay to have more time in the sun.

The Magic Scythe

READER 2:
    That wasn't all, she was also known to hire men for haying;
    Then on completion of the job, she'd dismiss them without paying.

READER 3:
    Unaware, this desperate man offered to do her haying;
    The woman accepted the offer, even warned him about not paying.

READER 1:
    Somehow the woman reconsidered, and proposed an unusual counter-offer:

WOMAN:
    If you're able to cut more grass in a five-day span than I can rake in one day;
    I'll be happy to reverse my decision and grant you five-day's pay.

READER 4:
    The man was happy to agree to the terms, and set about to work;
    The scythe that he'd been given—what an extraordinary perk!

READER 3:
    In five days of heavy mowing it remained as sharp as new;
    And the cutting was on schedule—four days now, and almost through!

READER 2:
    One day, entering the forge near the house, he saw scythes of all descriptions;
    He couldn't help but wonder

READER 1 (Man):
    Has this woman been having conniptions?

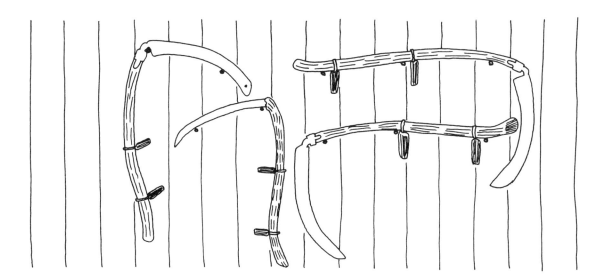

READER 4:

> To be quite honest, though, he had felt a strange sensation,
> Wondering whether beneath that veneer loomed powers of incantation.

READER 2:

> While the man slept, the elf-woman appeared again near morning,
> She spoke frankly in his dream—a word of dire warning.

ELF-WOMAN:

> There is no way in which you could mow more than the witch can rake;
> So when you discover that you're beaten go into the forge, and have your "take."
> Take scythe handles and blades, all you think you can use;
> Rush to the section of uncut hay, and you will get your dues.

READER 4:

> Next morning, remembering the dream, he surveyed the unmowed land;
> At six o'clock the witch came out—five rakes at her command.

READER 3:

> She spread the rakes on the hay, cackled some voodoo bits;
> The rakes spun into action, hay gathered in frenzying fits!

READER 1:

> Sure now of her unusual powers, the man snuck to the forge from his dream;
> Grabbed several handles, fit blades to them; on to a competing scheme!

READER 2:

> He took his cues from the elf-woman and laid the scythes on the grass;
> And would you believe the action—mowing took on real class!

READER 3:
> The witch's rakes couldn't keep pace with the assembled scythes cutting reams;
> The man was jubilant—blades "zinging" over the witch's screams.

READER 4:
> The witch gave him credit for his smarts; and offered more work gathering hay;
> Even gave him his room and board and a handsome increase in pay.

READER 2:
> Years passed, and eventually he took up his own piece of land;
> He found a wife who shared his work, just the two of them, hand in hand.

READER 4:
> He never failed to mow his grass; and always used the same scythe.
> Even shared the secret of it's magic,

READER 1:
> But only with his wife.

READER 3:
> The good wife promised she'd never, ever lend the scythe to her neighbours;
> It was a scythe that was strictly reserved for her and her husband's labours.

READER 1:
> Alas, one day the man went out to fish, and a neighbour came down the trail;
> He had no scythe, he had lost his own, spilled forth his tear-jerking tale.

READER 2:
> Disarmed, the wife, what could she do but give in to that tale of woe!
> Reluctantly, she caved in and let that magical implement go.

READER 3:
> She gave clear directions on what not to do, like temper the blade with fire;
> The man promised glibly.

READER 4 (Neighbour):
> Cross my heart.

READER 2:
> Then, turned out to be a liar.

READER 1:

The neighbour immediately set to work; and mowed with all his gut,
It didn't matter how hard he tried, the blade just wouldn't cut.

READER 3:

Angry now, he sharpened the blade, his mood was down in the mire;
When it failed to cut this time—off to the forge, and he gave it fire!

READER 4:

The moment the flames made contact, the blade melted down to a heap;
He dashed for the neighbours to find the wife, suspecting he was "in deep."

READER 3:

The woman dreaded her husband's wrath; indeed, there was a tirade;
But after a single outburst, he conceded;

READER 1 (Man):

It was only a blade.

READERS 1 & 2 :

The couple would live into old age, he would always remember the dream;

READERS 3 & 4:

But the loss, no longer an issue—the two lived in happiness supreme.

The Magic Scythe

A Cookie Mix and a Ginger Fix

A retelling of The Gingerbread Boy
- An American Tale -
(For **Eight Readers**)

READER 1:
>
> In a far-off land, long, long ago, A lonely old pair mixed a magical dough.

READER 2:
>
> They started with ginger in this fantastic batter;
> Shaped a boy-like cookie and placed him on a platter.

READER 3:
>
> They stuck him in the oven, and let the creature bake;
> Quite unaware, I'm sure, of this innocent mistake.

READER 1:
>
> They opened the oven door and found to their surprise—
> A hyper cookie creature with taunting raisin eyes.

READER 2:
>
> Not at all what they expected; a whoop and then a sigh;
> Was this creature doped on ginger, or on a sugar high?

READER 3:
>
> Without "hello" or a fond "good-bye," he streaked across the floor;

READER 2:
>
> No "please," or "thank you, Mom and Dad," he bolted through the door.

READER 1:
>
> The poor old couple was in shock that the tramp would **VAMOOSE!**
> So on their toes, this little pair pursued the guy on the loose.

OLD WOMAN:
>
> Stop, stop, you little scamp!

READER 2:
>
> She followed him in haste.

OLD WOMAN:
>I'm not about to let
>All that ginger go to waste!

GINGERBREAD BOY:
>Run, run, as fast as you can,
>I'm not your average gingerbread man!

READER 3:
>He out-ran the poor old lady with a burst of lighning speed;
>Even with the dear old man, G. B. maintained the lead.

READER 1:
>With a glint in his eye,
>Over his shoulder he shouted:

GINGERBREAD BOY:
>Run, run, dear little man!
>Try to catch me, if you can!

OLD MAN:
>I give up! This chase is absurd;
>I can't out-run that spiced-up nerd.

READER 2:
>G. B. thought he was out of the woods, no regrets of deceit or cheating;
>Then quickly caught by surprise, to hear a Nanny Goat's loud bleating.

NANNY GOAT:
>**STOP! STOP!** My little man,
>I'll catch you and eat you; I'm a fully-charged old Nan.

60

A Cookie Mix and a Ginger Fix

READER 3:

     The boy kept running, looked over his shoulder,

     And shouted, this time, even bolder:

GINGERBREAD BOY:

     Run, run, as fast as you can,

     I can out-run you, clumsy old Nan.

READER 1:

     As for the nanny, from the family, Gruff:

     She wasn't new to trick or bluff.

READER 2:

     She tried one of her bribes, a syrupy, "Hi!"

     You should have seen the ginger fly.

GINGERBREAD BOY

     Good try, my Nanny, just try again; no "ifs" or "butts" for this runaway man.

READER 3:

     A woman, a man, a Nanny goat, too,

     And then, in pursuit, a bellowing "MOO!"

READER 1:

     Poor G. B., what brought on this curse?

     Just read on, there's another verse.

GINGERBREAD BOY:

     Run, old cow, kick up your heels;

     I'm not a big favourite among bovine meals.

READER 2:

     The cow in the dust; then without delay,

     A pig showed up in this dizzying relay.

GINGERBREAD BOY:

> Run, run as your flab allows;
> I've out-run people, goats, and even cows.

READER 1:

> He came to a flowing stream, too wide for him to cross;
> Scratched his sugary head; "Now what!" G. B. at a loss.

READER 2:

> When out of the blue, to his utter surprise,
> A fox appeared—cunning in his eyes.

FOX:

> **YUM!** Do I smell spice?
> You may have heard tales, but I can be nice!
> Before you can say, "Fox Freedle" you'll be back on track.
> If all else fails, get on my back.

GINGERBREAD BOY:

> I'm getting desperate, they're on my trail.
> Sweet talk or not, I'm on your tail;

FOX:

> **Oh! Oh!** You know you're in trouble,
> Quick, get on my back, on the double!

READER 3:

> What choice? What woe!
> G.B. had nowhere else to go.

FOX:

> Move up, young man, the water's getting deeper;
> Perch on my nose, now; just trust your friendly keeper.

READER 1:

> G. B. now, no options left, straddled the fox's snout;
> A **SNIFF** and a **WHIFF** and a crunchy **SNAP!** G. B.'s light finally snuffed out!

READER 1, 2 & 3:

> What happened to the friendly couple still remains a myst'ry;
> As for poor G. B., just another page in hist'ry.

A Cookie Mix and a Ginger Fix

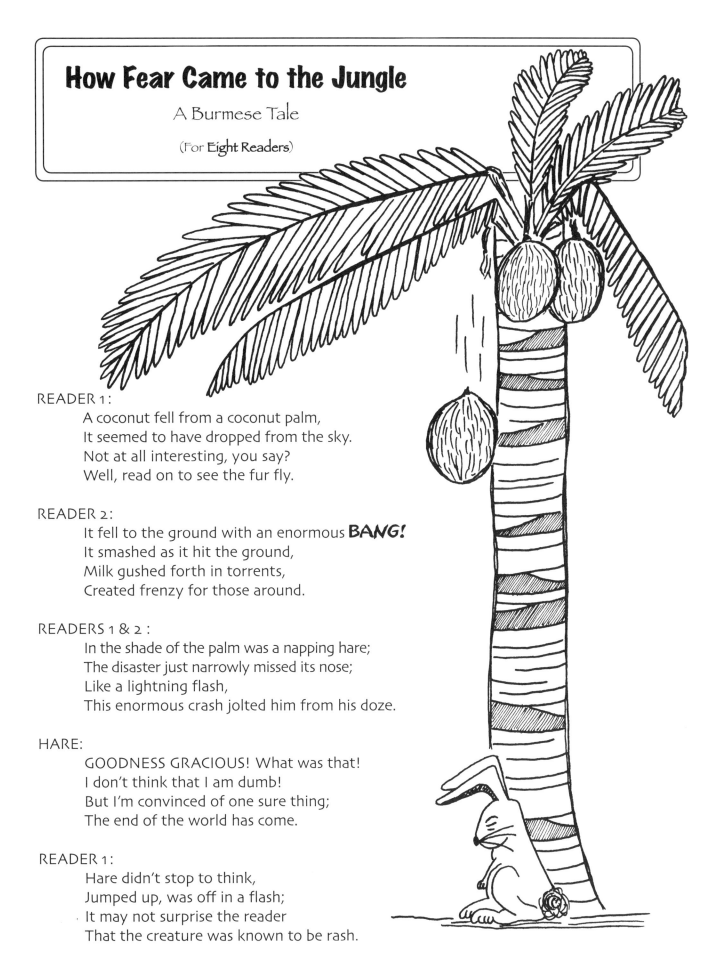

How Fear Came to the Jungle

A Burmese Tale

(For Eight Readers)

READER 1:

A coconut fell from a coconut palm,
It seemed to have dropped from the sky.
Not at all interesting, you say?
Well, read on to see the fur fly.

READER 2:

It fell to the ground with an enormous **BANG!**
It smashed as it hit the ground,
Milk gushed forth in torrents,
Created frenzy for those around.

READERS 1 & 2:

In the shade of the palm was a napping hare;
The disaster just narrowly missed its nose;
Like a lightning flash,
This enormous crash jolted him from his doze.

HARE:

GOODNESS GRACIOUS! What was that!
I don't think that I am dumb!
But I'm convinced of one sure thing;
The end of the world has come.

READER 1:

Hare didn't stop to think,
Jumped up, was off in a flash;
It may not surprise the reader
That the creature was known to be rash.

HARE:

> The end of the world has come—it comes as no surprise;
> Don't say I haven't warned you; just call me "Mr. Wise."

READER 2:

> And very soon, the clever hare met Jackal, a long-time friend;
> And told his friend the latest news—that the world was at its end.

JACKAL:

> I should very much have liked
> To see this once-in-a-life event;
> In any case, I'll warn my friends,
> Entertainment, my natural bent.
>
> And here comes Mr. Tortoise—
> Old "Slow Coach," with that lazy crawl;
> Though whether the world has come
> Or gone may not interest him at all.

HARE:

> I'm not going to speak to him; he's the rudest creature I know;
> He'll come up with sarcastic remarks when he hears about the "blow."

READERS 1 & 2:

> Hare was really a pretty good sort, though not especially smart;
> In breaking news like the "end of the world."

READER 1:

> But Jackal, of a different ilk, could not resist temptation;
> And called loudly for tortoise to hear about the fall of earth's creation.

JACKAL:

> You must hear the news I bring you ponderous, old slow poke;
> The world has come to a sudden end—this time, it's not a joke.

TORTOISE:

> **HUMPH!** I do declare, I've heard
> That the world could do such a thing;
> But there's nothing I can really do;
> Who knows what the day will bring?

READER 2:

> But all the same, he turned about to follow the other two,
> While he didn't seem to care a lot, with this news right out-of-the-blue.

How Fear Came to the Jungle

READER 1:

    And the three went nitter natter—as to who should get the news.
    There was Bear, Buffalo, and Cat—they had better choose.

JACKAL:

    I shouldn't worry about Cat—let's cut out all this chatter;
    Since she's known to have nine lives, one more or less won't matter.

HARE:

    It could well be she's on her ninth, and faces her final stint—
    I think that at the very least the creature deserves a hint.

READER 2:

    They made one firm decision—to tell Bear would be wise,
    He might be sensitive and retaliate; they'd better respect his size.

READER 1:

    But especially, they'd tell Buffalo wallowing in mud to his neck;
    It was Jackal's idea to tell him, but the threesome made the trek.

JACKAL:

    HEYA! HELLO! Old twisty tail, our news may come like a thud;
    The world has come to a sudden end—you don't want to get caught in that mud.

BUFFALO:

    To an end it's come? Did you say world! Which end? Is it up, down, or which?
    I'm going to step out of this mire—interrupt my bath! Oh, my itch!

READER 2:

    Jackal was really a cowardly type, he'd been cheeky, responding in fun.
    As to which end, he'd replied,

JACKAL:

    Well, it's the end you're standing on.

READER 1:

    Buffalo just moved right on—no response to the jibe;
    Spluttered out of the muck to warn the rest of the tribe.

FLY:

    BUZZ! BUZZ! What's all this fuss? At first I thought zebras had stormed;
    My worst fear of fears—that the bees had again swarmed.

JACKAL:

    BEES! How I wish that was all.
    The situation is worse, buzzy chum,
    Just hang on to your frizzy wings,
    My friend—the end of the world has come.

HARE:

> Hang on by your hairy feet, I know you don't have toes;
> This will be your safest escape; just do not tickle my nose.
>
> Your weight is no problem—I can do this with ease;
> But just one tickle from those feet, and you'll blow to bits with my sneeze.

FLY:

> Thank you, and thank you. What a surprise! We were just buzzing and humming—
> Completely oblivious that we'd learn that the end of the world was coming.

READER 2:

> Jackal lost no time at all; he'd become the new "doomcaster,"
> And soon all the jungle creatures were fleeing from impending disaster.

JACKAL:

> We have no recourse, no time to lose; his Majesty, the lion, must know
> About this terrible disaster—this dreadful tale of woe.

READER 1:

> And so it was that all agreed to search for the jungle monarch;
> And since Jackal was practiced in talking, he would let him out of the dark.

READER2:

> When they entered the royal presence they bowed with united accord;
> It was Jackal who raised his voice and announced the doom to their lord.

JACKAL:

> Oh, King of the Jungle, hear us out! We don't know what to do.
> The world has come to a sudden end, and it's left us all in a stew.

READERS 1 & 2 :

> The kingly beast just raised his head, and snorted:

LION:

> *BOSH!* and utter nonsense! **HO! HA!** and **HUMM!**
> I only demand to know one thing—who saw the ending come?

READER 1:

> This shook them all into a frenzy and eyes soon fixed on Hare;
> They pushed the poor thing forward—though not with nerve to spare.

READER 2:

> It was Jackal, who once more, opened his mouth to reply:

How Fear Came to the Jungle

JACKAL:

It was Hare who saw something dreadful falling out of the sky.

LION:

And how did Hare know that this meant the end of the world was here?
We know he isn't brilliant—I'm not at all convinced, I fear.

HARE:

If you please, your Majesty, I was under the coconut tree;
I fell asleep and was rudely awakened by this terrible crash near me.

When I awoke, I just bolted—though weary from my snooze;
I just rushed, and in a twitter brought Jackal the terrible news.

LION:

I SEE! That is, I think I see! I command you, Hare, no more pretend!
Lead us all, I say, to the very spot where the world came to an end.

READER 1:

The march was dreadful, it was long; none dared to make a sound;
And finally, they all arrived at the spot where a coconut lay on the ground.

READERS 1 & 2:

Hare came to a sudden stop and then the dreaded question:

LION:

Is that your world? **ARRRRRRRG!**

READER 2:

Lion's roar was so terrible it shook the leafy floor.
No one uttered as much as a sound—then another enormous **ROARRRR!**

HARE:

Your Majesty, please sir Majesty; I pray that you forgive this "bungle;"
As I have urgent business on the other side of the jungle.

READER 1:

And before as much as an ear was pricked or anyone engaged their brain,
Hare was off like an arrow, never to be seen again.

READERS 1 & 2:

Reminiscent of another story about a sky that had fallen;
Except those unlucky creatures—fell prey to a fox's callin'.

Turtle Stew—What's a Coyote to Do?

A retelling of the First Nation tale
(For *Six Readers*)

READER 1:

By now you know, that animals talk in tales,
This one, true to the pattern, begins with a turtle on the rails.

READER 2:

He was young and quite naïve[1] to crawl from his river home;
He needed water to survive –how would he dare to roam?

READER 3:

Turtle munched on delectable flies, slurped worms that pleasingly squished,
Didn't notice the heat and dust—had more than he'd ever wished.

READER 4:

The great circle we know as the Sun, climbed high above in the cerulean[2] sky,
And finally Turtle remembered—without the river, he'd fry.

READER 1:

Turtle dragged himself off the path, found shade 'neath a jagged rock,
Wailed and wept with wild abandon—quite unlike strains of Dvorak.[3]

TURTLE:

Oh, woe is me, it's so hot and dry,
I need water, good ol' H_2O, or surely I will die.

READER 2:

Now, notice here, turtle hadn't ventured far,
He merely moved without great haste, for that's how his kind are.

READER 3:

Not surprising, as tales will go, coyote happened to come by,
On the hunt for lunch—his attention peaked by the mournful cry.

---

1   naïve—having a natural simplicity and honesty
2   ce·ru·le·an—resembling the blue of the sky
3   Dvorák—(d&-)'vor-"zhāk, Czech composer
    [Note: Bartók could replace Dvorák in this verse, for ease of pronunciation
    Bartók, Hungarian pianist-composer.]

READER 4:

He sniffed the path, followed the sound, not feeling an ounce of compassion,
His only goal and heart's desire, to get his daily ration.

READER 1:

As quick as a wink, he spied Turtle cowering behind the rock;
To Turtle the sight of Coyote, inspired not dread, but shock.

COYOTE:

Dear Turtle,

READER 3:

Coyote began in a syrupy voice,

COYOTE:

Please teach me your sad song, or I will eat you whole; I'll simply have no choice.

READER 2:

Turtle had a hunch he would be lunch, whether he sang the song or not,
A nervous quiver ran under his shell; he felt quite queasy and hot.

READER 4:

He knew he needed a plan, to outwit the hungry Coyote,
And he was cleverer than he was fast—that would be my vote.

READER 1:

Turtle wrapped his brain around a plan, looked Coyote straight in the eye,

TURTLE:

   If you swallow me shell and all, you will surely die.

COYOTE:

   Oh, I see that might be true; so teach me your mournful song,
   Or I will leave you to boil in the blazing sun, no qualms about what I've done.

READER 3:

   Turtle guffawed and briefly stated:

TURTLE:

   I'm not worried one iota, my thick shell will save my skin,
   Whether here or in South Dakota.

READER 2:

   About to blow his top, Coyote had one last idea to deliver,
   Mouth watering beyond control;

COYOTE:

   I will toss you into the river.

TURTLE:

   The river. No, not the river! That's what I fear the most;
   I'll drown; I'll be toast; I'll be a green-shelled ghost.

READER 4:

   Coyote was fast, but not too swift.

READER 1:

   (He couldn't think on his feet);

Turtle Stew—What's a Coyote to Do?

READER 2:

So with one last threat,

COYOTE:

Sing or swim?

READER 3:

Turtle shrivelled in defeat.

READER 4:

One terrific heave and splash, Coyote felt he had won the day;
So what if there was no Turtle stew, at least that creature was out of the way.

READER 1:

But as Coyote turned to leave, a teasing, goading laugh was heard
Made him cringe and made him groan, Turtle would have the final word.

TURTLE:

In this river I was born, here, too, I was bred,
It's here I swim all day, and at night make my bed.

READER 2:

Tail between his legs, poor Coyote felt insecure,
Realizing he'd been had, by what was to have been his "soup de jour."

Wild Superstitions and Street Musicians

A retelling of The Bremen Town Musicians
- A German Tale -
(For **Seven Readers**)

READER 1:
> A special donkey had spent long years hauling bags of grain to be milled;
> One day he heard faint murmers that he was about to be killed.

READER 2:
> His master had noted signs that Donkey was dragging his feet;
> And now had fears about the cost of food he'd continue to eat.

READER 3:
> Donkey had no recourse but to escape from this cruel man;
> He took to the road with haste, to devise an alternate plan.

DONKEY:
> While my legs are getting weary, I must get on the draw;
> My singing voice is strong—**HEE HAW, HEE HAW, HEE HAW!**
> I could join the street musicians—so to speak, as the final straw!

READER 1:
> On his way to the nearest city, a dog lay in his path;
> Weary, run down, and panting, it had escaped its owner's wrath.

DOG:
> I used to be a hunting dog, but then my legs gave out;
> My master connived, this way and that, to bring my demise about.

DONKEY:
> Listen to me, my hairy friend, I'm on my way to the city;
> You and I will make a handsome duo, as we chant our little ditty.

DOG:
> Oh, I can sing a ditty, and how! **BOW WOW! BOW WOW! BOW WOW!**

READER 2:
> And soon the two were on their way to launch a new vocation;
> With a **HEE HAW HAW** and a **BOW WOW WOW** in a spirit of jubilation.

READER 3:

    They hadn't gone far when they met a cat at the end of its tether;
    Bleary-eyed, and a face as long as three days of rainy weather.

DONKEY:

    Just to look at you I'd say you're in a troubled condition;
    How would you like to join us to become a city street musician?

CAT:

    Indeed, I'm a troubled old Tom; teeth too dull to kill mice;
    My owner wants to drown me now; a thought that's far from nice!

DONKEY & CAT:

    You look like our kind; just join our show;
    Come on, off to the city where we'll go, go, go!

CAT:

    I'm sure I'll blend with all this **HEE HAW, BOW WOW WOW;**
    I've been known to handle a fancy line—**MEOWW, MEOWW, MEOWW!**

READER 1:

    So the three trudged on till they came to a farm—
    To welcome another member—preferably one with charm.

READER 2:

    Indeed, there he was, in deep distress, a giant had-been rooster;
    His red comb hanging down to his knees, obviously in need of a booster.

DONKEY:

    No need to explain, it's obvious you're no longer in the loop;
    There must have been family whisperings about your place in Sunday's soup.

CAT & DOG:

    This is our invitation for you to join this august troupe;
    To blend with our voices—the cackling sensation of our group.

ROOSTER:

    I have a lot to crow about; in spite of the farmer's to-do;
    I trained each morning for years, **Cockadoodle DOO DOO DOO!**

READER 3:

    Tired, the foursome trudged on—about time to start counting sheep;
    So, weary from a long day's trek they settled down to sleep.

READER 1:

    The rooster flew to the top of a tree, to keep watch for intruders, you see;
    The rest of the motley animal crew were soon asleep beneath the tree.

READER 2:

    But it wasn't long till Rooster announced that he'd seen a light—
    There must be a house there, a more comfortable place for the night.

READER 3:

    They soon were up and on their way to check the source of light;
    They moved with caution and fear in the darkness of the night.

READER 1:

    The light soon led the troupe to a house on a city street;
    Exhausted and hungry, the musicians rested their weary feet.

READER 2:

    A light at this late hour brought suspicion to the four;
    Up on his hind legs, Donkey decided to check the "score."

READER 3:

    The most amazing things he saw—guns and knives galore;
    Lots of food left on the table—and chests of gold on the floor.

ROOSTER:

    I could do with some food after our strenuous beat!

DOG:

    You can say that again—I think I smell meat.

CAT:

　　It would be like a dream to get a taste of cream.

DONKEY:

　　You're moving too fast, there may be robbers inside;
　　If we don't use our smarts we could lose our hides.

DONKEY, ROOSTER, DOG & CAT:

　　Right on! Ours smarts indeed! Let's quickly devise a scheme!
　　We'll shout in a mighty chorus and shatter every beam.

READER 1:

　　Donkey, once more pawed the window ledge;
　　Dog hopped up on his back;
　　The beginning of an animal ladder
　　Ready for a musical attack.

READER 2:

　　Cat leapt up, hung onto Dog,
　　Rooster perched on Cat's tail;
　　Poised for a mighty cacophony,
　　A plan that would not fail.

READER 3:

　　At Donkey's signal, the music began—
　　Meowing, crowing, and braying;
　　Then barking—till louder and louder
　　The structure was teetering and swaying.

READER 2:

　　The robbers were spooked by this prodigious musical din;
　　They had visions of goblins and ogres—terrified out of their skin.

READER 1:

　　With the speed of a prairie blizzard, they vacated their cozy spot;
　　Took off for the woods, terror had struck the lot.

READER 3:

　　The musicians rushed in to enjoy a remarkable feast;
　　A repast far beyond expectations of the average farmyard beast.

READER 1:

　　With full stomachs, the animals settled in, though somewhat bloated;
　　Their scheme had been a success—as they mused and gloated.

Readers Theatre

DONKEY:
I'll just settle on a bit of this straw;

DOG:
I'll hunker down on the mat;

ROOSTER:
I'll take a place on the shelf;

CAT:
I belong near the stove,

READER 2:
Meowed Cat.

READER 3:
MEANWHILE. . .

READER 1:
Back in the woods, the robber chief, with caution and doubt,
Appointed the bravest rogue to check their former hideout.

READER 2:
In the black of night he entered the house, with sniffers as keen as a rat;
He struck up a light, only to kindle the great fiery eyes of the cat.

READER 3:
Cat, in mid-air, spat at his face; Dog made a vicious attack;
A kick from Donkey, a crow from Rooster—the rogue would never come back.

READER 1:
He dashed with dispatch, in the belief—that a witch had scratched his face;

READER 2:
Had suffered a blow from a giant's wood leg—an ego scarred;

READER 3:
What utter disgrace!

READERS 1, 2 & 3:
The happy foursome had won the day—resided in posh conditions;
As for their earlier hopes and dreams—no need to become musicians.

Beanstalk Chronicles

A retelling of Jack and the Beanstalk

(For **Seven Readers**)

READER 1:

Jack, his mother, and a fine milk cow lived many years ago.
Milk and bread was all they had, ragged from head to toe.

READER 2:

One morning, during early chores Jack heard his mother cry:

MOTHER:

 Come quick, my lad, and you will see, our only cow's gone dry.
How will we manage, my dear boy, when prices are sky high?

JACK:

 Don't worry, mother, you will find, this cow is worth a mint;
I'll take her into town, I will and bring you every cent.

READER 3:

If only Jack had used his head, he would have foreseen danger;

READER 2:

Too bad, he ignored Red Riding Hood's tough lesson from a stranger.

READER 1:

Jack, indeed, did meet a stranger, not the furry kind, I vow;
But one who offered Jack some beans in trade for his white cow.

READER 2:

In some ways Jack was worldly wise, the stranger, oh, so shrewd;
He fed Jack a convincing line; Jack listened to the dude.

READER 3:

To trade five beans for a family cow, took nerve, or desperation;

READER 1:

Whichever of the two it was, Jack gave in to the man's persuasion.

MOTHER:

 I see you've parted with the cow, so, how much did she bring?
I don't much like the look you've got – what's up, you ding-a-ling?

JACK:

 You won't believe the bargain, mom, the loss at first seems tragic.
But I have a pocketful of beans, and they will sprout like magic.

READER 2:

Poor mother was beside herself; she screamed, she flailed, she frowned;

READER 3:

She chewed Jack out with venom, beans scattered on the ground.

READER 1:

Jack went to bed, he had no choice; then had the wildest dreams;
Of beanstalks reaching to the sky, sheer magic, so it seems.

READER 2:

When he awoke, he was surprised; leaves pressed against the glass;
He jumped from his pyjamas,

READERS 1 & 2:

That stranger was first class!

READER 3:

No time to waste, he climbed right up the beanstalk to its tip;
He saw a house and entered, to rest from the strangest trip.

READER 1:

A woman met him at the door, with no great enthusiasm,

GIANTESS:

I'll warn you child, my giant husband could gulp you in one spasm.
This place is not for puny kids,
Quickly take your bean route down or your life will be on skids.

JACK:

I'm starved, I'm famished; I left without my breakfast;
If I take leave on that tall beanstalk I know that I can't last.

READER 3:

What dreadful timing!

READER 1:

A thump outside the door,

READER 3:

The woman knew beyond a doubt the poor kid's likely score.

READER 2:

No time to think or scheme, but in one miraculous heave,
Tossed the kid into the oven, no chance that he would leave.

GIANT:

Fee-fi-fo-fummy! You may think that I'm a dumby!
I may not know where he is from, but I'll hunt him down, the little scum!

GIANTESS:

Poor man, I know that your hunger pangs have gotten to your head.
Just have a little patience and breakfast will be fed.

READER 3:

What sway this woman had with charm and a presence of wit;
But when she saw the kid's nose out, she dissolved into a snit.

GIANTESS:

SHHHHH! Don't leave until you hear the most prodigious snoring,
That's your only chance, my son to escape a sure-fire goring.

READER 1:

    It wasn't long before Jack felt the house in a violent shake;
    This was his cue, at last for a terrifying break.

READER 2:

    He tiptoed from the giant's house without a nod or smile;
    He slid along the beanstalk for what seemed at least a mile.

JACK:

     I'm home, dear Mom, I have some gold;
    I've made the grandest trade, though I'll admit that I was bold.

MOTHER:

     Gold, dear son, real gold, dear son, I don't know what to say;
    What a reward for a cow gone dry, let's live it up today.

READER 3:

    And that's exactly what they did, no thought of flood or drought;
    Before you could utter, "Beanie Brain," the gold had all run out.

READER 1:

    The only evidence of their fortune—the beanstalk near the shack;
    Poor Jack ascended one more time, risk of impending attack.

READER 2:

    The giant woman's greeting now was anything but kind;
    Apparently the missing gold freaked out the giant's mind.

JACK:

     Good morning, Mum, I know it's odd that I should dared to have come back;
    But all that's left of what I stole is this, the empty sack.

READER 3:

    No sooner had he made the plea, a thump, both fierce and huge;
    The woman offered one more heave to the former, warm refuge.

GIANT:

     Fee-fi-fo-fum! You may think that I've gone nuts!
    I know there's someone in the house, and I will have his guts.

GIANTESS:

     Fee, fi, and fiddle-dee-dee, there's no one here as you can see.
    Have your sausage and your bacon, I'll admit last time you were taken.

    Beanstalk Chronicles

READER 1:

Once more the ogre was appeased with words and food, I'm told;
He whistled down the morsels, his mind, this time on gold.

GIANT:

Come magic hen, I'm quite impatient for you to lay an egg;
Just drop the gold, I pray—I'm in no mood to beg.

READER 2:

The egg dropped with a rich cling, clang! The giant began to snore;
Jack made one leap for the magic hen, high-tailed it for the door.

READER 3:

This time not as lucky as he had been before.
The hen began to cackle just outside the door.

READER 1:

Jack headed for the beanstalk, just in the nick of time;
The giant was outraged now, intent to avenge the crime.

READER 2:

Jack and his Mom were happy, more gold than enough, indeed;
Though a rags to riches transformation often ends in greed.

READER 3:

That certainly was the case with these two heirs of wealth.
Jack scaled the beanstalk one more time, with caution, even stealth!

READER 1:

He found his way into the house; no sooner was he hidden;
He heard a thunderous

ALL:

THUMP! THUMP! THUMP!

READER 1:

And angry words, no kiddin'.

GIANT:

I've had enough of this impudent lad, **Fee-fi-fo and a fumy, FUMM! FUMM!**
I'll hunt him down; I know he's here, He's taking me for dumb.
By beef or by bacon, I'm not going to be taken.

Readers Theatre

GIANTESS:

 Look in the oven—that's his spot; whenever he appears,
Just grab the little scoundrel; I've had it to my ears!

READER 2:

Once more Jack succeeded to outwit the giant pair;
His greed had taken over—the boy had nerve to spare.

READER 3:

He knew the giant would fall asleep, a pattern he could predict;
He'd wait him out; easy stuff! He had the system licked.

READER 1:

He listened for the giant's snore, a harp he heard instead.
Not just any old harp, but a harp of gold; greed gripped his heart of lead.

JACK:

 I'll wait in here till this old goon dozes off once more;
I'll dart right for the beanstalk and let the ogre snore.

READER 2:

No sooner had he grabbed the harp and headed for the legume;
And then a roar that shook the house, a giant in a **FUME**.

READER 3:

The harp refused its gentle strains, instead shrieked for its master;
With lightning speed, Jack slid down; just barely escaped disaster.

READER 1:

Back to his senses, and not too soon, Jack hollered as he slid,
For Mom to grab the family axe and hand it to her kid.

READER 2:

The race was on, too close for Jack; the axe in hands aquiver;
Good rhyme predicts the outcome—the giant succumbed his liver.

READER 3:

Fairy tales, so it's said, should have a happy ending;
For Jack and Mom, this was the case; for giants the rules need bending.

READERS 1, 2 & 3:

Jack's final fortune, it is said, was to find a royal maid:
A hen supplied them all their lives with the golden eggs she laid.

Trouble About—A Witch Snuffed Out

A retelling of Hansel and Gretel—A German Tale
(For **Eight Readers**)

READER 1:

    The story is told of a woodchopper, and a wife with a heart of leather;
    Two children whom only Dad adored—a man at the end of his tether.

READER 2:

    Their food supply was running short, drought, and perhaps inflation;
    The parents reached a breaking point, a peak in their frustration.

WOODCHOPPER:

    No work, no food, what can we do—poor starving little kids!

STEPMOTHER:

    We'll take them to the forest; put the poor waifs on skids.

    Let's take them when morning breaks, at six, or even seven;
    This place without those children will be like seventh heaven.

READER 3:

    The nasty woman disliked children; she had a cruel bent;
    Aware of forest dangers, she had a heart of cement.

READER 1:

    Poor children lay awake that night, stomachs like empty sacks;
    They heard the conversation—stepmom's cruel attacks.

HANSEL:

    Trust me, sister, I'm very brave; please remember that!
    There's more than just one way to skin a wicked cat.

READER 2:

    Hansel was a cunning lad, the moon was shining bright;
    He gathered pebbles for their trek, not in the least uptight.

READER 3:

Poor kids, to think their mother was planning their final fate;
They'd barely closed their eyes, it seemed, when she barked at them,

STEPMOTHER:

 It's late!

WOODCHOPPER:

 We're off to the forest to gather wood for our fire;
We need an early start, I say, our lot is truly dire.

STEPMOTHER:

 Come along, you little tramps, before the sky turns grey;
Here's a tiny piece of bread—that's all there is today.

READER 1:

And so the four were on their way; only Hansel lagged behind;
He slyly laid his clever plan—the path with pebbles lined.

READER 2:

They wandered far into the woods, when mother bade them rest;
Hansel resisted all temptation to get things off his chest.

READER 3:

The children offered no resistance, pretended to be duped;
If you really want the truth—the two of them were pooped.

READER 1:

The older two just wandered on; pretending they'd come back;
The direction they were heading was clearly toward the shack.

READER 2:

The sun was setting in the west when Gretel began to weep;
Though with Hansel's consolation she soon would fall asleep.

READER 3:

Bright moonlight flooded the once dark wood; the children soon awoke.
Hansel saw the silver pebbles; no fear that they would croak.

HANSEL:

 Let's take this silvr'y path right to the cottage door;
And see the look on stepmom's face—she thought she knew the score.

Trouble About—A Witch Snuffed Out

GRETEL:

Let's hurry then, and find our way; let's not lose any time;
Don't you think, dear brother, desertion is a crime?

READER 1:

The path was clear right to the shack; the parents were in shock!
Father danced in utter glee—for once, mom couldn't talk.

READER 2:

Things seemed okay, just for awhile; and then the same old tune.
Food was getting scarce; the conniving started soon.

READER 3:

Again the parents took the kids, outfitted with some bread.
Hansel tried his former scheme, resorted to crumbs instead.

READER 1:

There's nothing that's especially new except for one detail;
Birds discovered the bread crumbs and cleared the forest trail.

GRETEL:

What shall we do, dear Hansel? Our path's become obscure;
I don't know how much more of this I'm able to endure.

READER 2:

And then to their surprise and joy a bird got their attention;
It urged the two to follow—an old fairy tale convention.

READER 3:

They came upon a cottage—what a glorious array of sweets!
Hansel grabbed a cookie—the two just gorged on treats.

READER 1:

But not for long—a voice, a voice as sweet as candy canes;
And to this day that syrupy voice strikes terror in their brains.

WITCH:

 Nibble, nibble, little mouse!
I'm missing candy from my house!

GRETEL & HANSEL:

It's nothing but a gentle breeze,
You may have heard a stirring in the trees.

READER 2:

But something was wrong as both of them feared,
When through the window a witch appeared.

WITCH:

 Come closer, dear children; I'll be happy to help you;
Please step inside and I'll feed you two.

READER 3:

Poor Hansel was easily taken in—Gretel much less keen;
That ugly face, that cackling laugh—shades of Hallowe'en!

READER 1:

She was an ugly sight, indeed as nearer the two she slithered;
A pointed nose, a protruding chin—a face all creased and withered.

READER 2:

She featured three of the longest teeth and a shrivelled, bristly chin;
It is no exaggeration to say—she was uglier than sin.

READER 3:

Reluctantly they followed her, their eyes popped open wide;
More treats were on the table once they were both inside.

READER 1:

While the two were snacking the witch made up their beds;
Getting the place all set for two weary "over-feds."

WITCH:

 Sleep tight, dear bunnies; a spell of peaceful slumber!
Aha! Those crazy little tots don't know I've got their number!

READER 2:

> The witch kept watch over the dozing pair; with the wickedest, toothiest grin;
> Visions of a gourmet meal—drool dripping from her chin.

READER 3:

> Their slumber was disturbed by the witch's piercing screams.
> She yanked the two right from their beds, aborted their peaceful dreams.

WITCH:

> Get up you lazy bones, get up you two! There's no time to waste;
> I'll stick you in the goose coop, boy; get in there now, make haste!
>
> As for you, my little girl, you'll help me with my work;
> We'll fatten up your brother, a task you'd rather shirk.

GRETEL:

> Oh, do take pity on two lost orphans who've simply lost their path;
> We'll never again disturb you, there's no reason for your wrath.

READER 1:

> The witch just glowered at the girl, pretended she hadn't heard;
> Then went about her business; her feelings quite unstirred.

READER 2:

> Day after day, the old witch checked for fat on Hansel's hand;
> The boy tricked her with old dry bones held out on demand.

READER 3:

> The witch's patience finally gave; she gave the girl a shout;
> Ordered heated water her secret all but out.

WITCH:

> Before we cook my supper, I want to do some baking;
> Please poke your head into the oven—and girl, please stop that shaking.

READER 1:

> The girl about to follow orders heard a bird somewhere.
> She heard it chirp, "Beware! Beware! Don't stick your head in there!"

READER 2:

> Gretel did collect her senses; and called the witch's bluff;
> She made a plea of ignorance about cooking and such stuff.

GRETEL:

Show me how I should proceed
With this important feat;
I'll follow suit if you show me
How to check the heat.

WITCH:

You silly girl, there's nothing to it;
Your head goes in like this!
I'll show you how it's done,
And then it's your turn, Miss!

READER 3:

The witch stuck in her ugly head; then Gretel in one quick swoop
Pushed her into the oven—took off for Hansel's coop.

READER 1:

Gretel's juices were now flowing her eyes ablaze with fire;
Her timing had been perfect; just beneath the wire!

GRETEL:

We're free, dear brother, free at last; there's nothing left to do;
The witch is inside cooking in a space designed for you.

READER 2:

The birds were hovering over the house, at least that's what's been said;
They showered the kids with precious gems, in thanks for crumbs of bread.

READER 3:

There are stories about their lot; among others, we are told
That they met a swan who gently embraced them in her fold.

READERS 1, 2 & 3 :

No prince, no princess in this ending; just one more thing is said:
The father was elated—poor stepmom has since fled.

Trouble About—A Witch Snuffed Out

Little Miss Fickle Caught in a Pickle

A retelling of The Three Bears

(For **Seven Readers**)

READER 1:

> Father, mother and a wee bear cub, lived in a forest shack;
> Happy threesome, hidden in trees, free from fear of attack.

MOTHER BEAR:

> Breakfast is ready, though just a tad hot;
> Let's wait a spell and cool the pot.

FATHER BEAR:

> Come mother, come little one; leave the door ajar;
> Just a quick, brisk walk, no need to go far.

BABY BEAR:

> A beautiful morning! What a great spot.
> Let's take our time while our breakfast is hot.

READER 2:

> So, off they went for a morning stroll, to let their porridge cool;
> Along came a girl named Goldilocks—why wasn't she in school!

READER 3:

> Silently tiptoed up the steps, she caught a whiff of porridge;
> She bolted through the unlocked door, a bundle of blatant courage.

READER 1:

> She looked around from room to room and found to her surprise,
> As she came into the kitchen, breakfast before her eyes.

GOLDILOCKS:

> *Ouch!* Good gracious! This bowl is much too hot;
> I'll try the next down the line—in fact, I'll try the lot.

READER 2:

> Baby's porridge, the smallest bowl, was completely to her taste;
> She wolfed it down in utter glee, then left the room in haste.

(Some, or even all, of the readers' parts may be read by a duet or small chorus)

GOLDILOCKS:

I'll look around this quaint old place, I'm eager to explore;
But as I do, I'll certainly keep, one eye fixed on the door.

READER 3:

She then sat down on the largest chair, but found it much too hard;
Then slipped into the middle-sized one, no longer on her guard.

GOLDILOCKS:

Oh, there's another, just my size; a wee little baby chair;
OOPS! OUCH! BOO HOO HOO!

READER 1:

Goldie's feet way up in the air.

READER 2:

Tears of anger, perhaps some pain; no concern for the ruined chair;
She bounded up the bedroom stairs, to look around up there.

GOLDILOCKS:

What a morning I have had! I'll stretch out on this bed.
But this is really much too hard; I'll try the next instead.

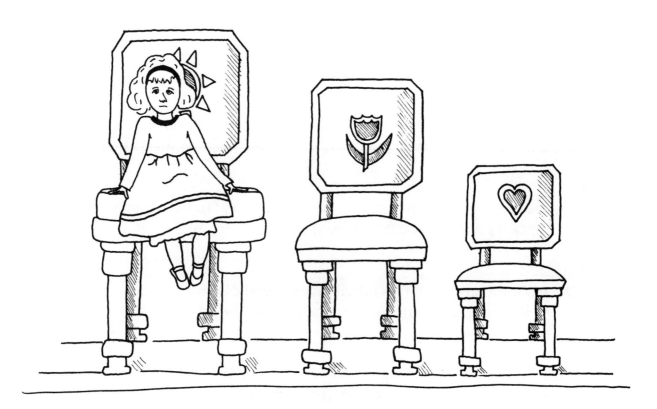

Little Miss Fickle Caught in a Pickle

READER 3:

    From one bed to another, lazily she moved;
    Again, it was the baby's property, of which she soon approved.

GOLDILOCKS:

    I'll just take a rest—no more than a minute, or so;
    All I need is forty winks, and then I'd better go.

READER 2:

    She wheezed, she snored, she was completely out!
    She would've had grim nightmares, had she heard of bears about.

READER 1:

    Meanwhile, there was the porridge, by this time, lumpy and cold;
    That's what the bears discovered— you should have heard them scold.

FATHER BEAR:

    I have a hunch, that strong left-elbow feeling,
    That there's something going on, that will send me through the ceiling!

    Who it might be is less than clear; I've heard of the beanstalk prankster;
    I hope it's not that huffing wolf—that insidious, prowling gangster.

BABY BEAR:

    BOOHOOHOO! It's not the wolf, though, indeed, a hungry soul;
    The evidence lies clearly, in my empty porridge bowl.

READER 2:

    The bears were in a terrible state—then Father slyly nudged his mate:

FATHER BEAR:

    Now look here, my sweet! Someone's been sitting in my seat.

READER 1:

    The puzzle cleared up bit by bit, as they went about their inspection;
    Mother Bear's chair was quite intact, poor Baby's a splintered collection.

READER 2:

But this time Baby had a fit when he heard an enormous snore;
The threesome made a beeline, straight for the upper floor.

FATHER BEAR:

Someone's been sleeping in my bed, her treatment will be less than tender;

READER 3:

The mystery till this day remains—where he got the scoop on gender.

READER 1:

MEANWHILE ...

MOTHER BEAR:

Someone has been lying here; someone other than you, my dear.

READER 2:

And then! A terrible tremor in the flooring:
The prodigious vibes of someone snoring.

BABY BEAR:

BOOHOO! BOOHOO! BOOHOOHOO! My word! My foot! My little hat!
Someone's sleeping in my bed; **BOOHOOHOO!** Who is that?

READER 3:

On two's and four's the parents dashed; they were in a terrible snit;
But by the time they reached the bed, Miss Goldilocks had split.

Readers 1, 2, and 3:

She flew down the stairs, as fast as the west wind blows,
Never to return to the place again, at least, so the story goes.

Troll Bluff and Billy Goat Stuff

A retelling of The Three Billy Goats Gruff

(For *Six Readers*)

READER 1:

Three Billy Goats Gruff, so the story goes,
Set out for a hill where the green grass grows.

READER 2:

On their way to the hill was a bridge with a toll;
A bridge dutifully guarded by a wicked old troll.

READER 1:

TRIP TRAP TRIP TRAP over the bridge they trotted;
TRIP TRAP TRIP TRAP unaware that they'd been spotted.

TROLL:

> What noise is that? Stop in your tracks;
> **No TRESSPASSING!** Not even for Billy Goat snacks.

BILLY GOAT 1:

> I'm Billy Goat One; I'm here with my brothers.
> I'd have sent Number Two if I'd had my druthers.

TROLL:

> What a good line dear little kid;
> You'll have to try harder or you'll lose your lid.

BILLY GOAT 1:

> I wouldn't make much of a lunch; I'm the tiniest, you see;
> My brother is coming soon, he's perfect for your tea.

TROLL:

> Smart little Billy, be off then, you goat!
> I'll be ready to get your brother by the throat.

READER 2:

> Over the bridge, then and up the steep hill
> Number one trotted to have his fill.
>
> **TRIP TRAP TRIP TRAP** Number Two, somewhat unnerved
> By the grim prospect he might soon be served.

TROLL:

> I heard you were coming—here's news for you my friend.
> My next serving for tea will mark your butting end.

BILLY GOAT 2:

> I'm Billy Goat Two joining my brother for lunch;
> Though it's clear to me now you already had a hunch.

TROLL:

> I've been through your brother's excuses and wails;
> I'm pretty steeped in strange fairy tales.
>
> I know how it goes—you'll wear me out,
> Convincing me that there's another about.

Troll Bluff and Billy Goat Stuff

BILLY GOAT 2:

    You're right on the mark—a tale without fallacy;

    It's a well-known fact that Number Three's a rare delicacy.

TROLL:

    You're smarter than the average goat; just be off and join your brother;

    I'll play by the rules of fairy tales—**BOSH! BOO HOO!** and **BLOTHER!**

READER 2:

    Billy Goat Two was off with gusto and delight.

    Before you could say Bill Goatson the goat was out of sight.

READER 1:

    TRIP TRAP TRIP TRAP Number Three's off to the slaughter!

    Then, before his very eyes the troll comes from the water.

TROLL:

    I've seen both brothers and I'm in a sour mood;

    I know there is no number four—so now's the time for food.

READER 2:

    Poor Troll remembered only part of that old, old tale;

    He assumed that his wily scheme simply couldn't fail.

BILLY GOAT 3:

    You know who I am –and you're in for a duel;

    You're about to be **TRIP TRAPPING** right into that pool!

TROLL:

    Poor butting Billy you must be bluffing;

    I've been waiting all day to have your stuffing.

BILLY GOAT 3:

    Here I am you ugly troll, all set for a royal duel;

    And then it's up to the grassy hill with my brothers to re-fuel.

READER 1:

    No time was lost; Billy stamped and butted,

    If you know the tale at all, the troll was all but gutted.

THREE BILLY GOATS:

    We're three little Billy Goats—crafty, smart, and free;

    These hills are ours with grass galore, more than enough for tea.

Hofus, The Stonecutter

A retelling of the Japanese Tale
(For **Five Readers**)

READER 1:

    Nobody remembers exactly when—let's just say, a long time back,
    A humble stonecutter in far off Japan lived in a mountain shack.

READER 2:

    Everyday the man would go to the mountain: across crags, into caves,
    For just the right rock from which to fashion stones to mark people's graves.

READER 3:

    There were stories Hofus had heard (That was the stonecutter's name)
    Of a mountain spirit with glorious powers, though no proof for the claim.

READER 1:

    One day Hofus delivered his wares to a home of wealth supreme;
    The glitter and opulence overshadowed imagination, even his wildest dream.

READER 2:

    As Hofus returned to his shack and thought of his lowly lot,
    He couldn't imagine a life of wealth, but longed to give it a shot!

STONECUTTER:

    How I'd love those silken curtains to surround me in my sleep;
    Those golden tassels and the finest rugs, and jewels in one big heap.

SPIRIT OF THE MOUNTAIN:

    Your fervent wish has been heard beyond the highest mountains;
    You shall have jewels and gems and glittering golden fountains.

READER 3:

    Hofus picked up his tools and headed for his shed;
    To find no humble shack, but a palace of gold instead.

STONECUTTER:

    I am the happiest man alive. I'll bask in this new-found glory.
    Carving stone and other chores will become a forgotten story.

READER 1:

And so it was that Hofus basked in gold and all things fancy;
But it was only a matter of days before he again turned antsy.

READER 2:

Summer came and the blazing sun made Hofus gasp for air;
The man decided to stay at home protected from the glare.

READER 3:

From his window he saw a carriage drawn by servants in silver and blue;
And a prince with a golden umbrella fanned by a servant crew.

STONECUTTER:

If only I could be a prince with servants at my side;
I know that I would be content—the happiest man worldwide.

SPIRIT OF THE MOUNTAIN:

Your wish is granted at this moment; a prince, indeed, you are;
You'll have a gold umbrella and servants from near and far.

READER 1:

A prince he was with all the grandeur that princely offices hold;
Servants clad in silver and blue, and an umbrella of 100K gold.

READERS 1, 2 & 3:

BUT THAT WAS NOT ENOUGH!

READER 2:

While walking through the garden his flowers were parched in the sun;
This in spite of the generous watering the servants had just done.

READER 3:

To add to his annoyance, Hofus sweltered in the shimmering blaze;
His annoyance turned to anger—caught in the dizzying haze.

Readers Theatre

STONECUTTER:

> The sun is mightier than a prince; how happy I would be
> If only I could replace the sun with disgruntled poor old me.

SPIRIT OF THE MOUNTAIN:

> Mountain spirit has heard your plea; again, your wish is granted;
> You can direct your beams this way or that—down and over—even slanted.

READER 1:

> Soon the fields of rice and grain
> Were seared in the blazing sun;
> There were scorched faces of princes and peasants
> From the mighty deeds he'd done.

READER 2:

> And then a cloud covered his face
> And hid the earth from him;
> How could a cloud have such might,
> To cause the world to dim!

STONECUTTER:

> A cloud mightier than the sun? that's something I find strange;
> But if that's the way things are, it's time I had a change.

SPIRIT OF THE MOUNTAIN:

> Once more, dear man, your wish is heard; a floating cloud you'll be;

READER 3:

> Another answer from the spirit, to yet another plea.

READER 1:

> The earth once more took on new life; lush growth and fresh clean air;
> But rain kept pouring all day long—there was water everywhere.

READER 2:

> Towns and villages were submerged, water stretched far and wide;
> Only one thing remained in tact—the rock on the mountain side.

READERS 1, 2 & 3:

> **NOW WHAT IS THERE LEFT TO WISH FOR?**

STONECUTTER:

> A rock, the mightiest of the lot! That comes as the wildest shock!
> Do I dare to breathe another wish, and risk being turned to rock?

Hofus, The Stonecutter

SPIRIT OF THE MOUNTAIN:

Once again, your wish is granted—you couldn't wish for more;
Safe in the sun and even rain; you're solid to the core.

READER 3:

There was happiness at last, though not for very long;
There was a tapping down below, tapping, steady and strong.

READERS 1, 2 & 3:
NOW WHAT?

READER 1:

After more tapping and some scraping—a continuous, annoying sound;
And then, to the rock's consternation, a slab fell to the ground.

STONECUTTER:

A man is mightier than a rock? I'd love to be a man;
With tools and might and energy, and a brain to create and plan.

SPIRIT OF THE MOUNTAIN:

You have your wish to be a man—enough of blues and mutter;
The best you can wish for, dear Hofus, to return to your life as a cutter.

READER 2:

And so it was, and so it continued—a stonecutter—he'd ask no more!

READER 3:

Contentment through creating things—it had all been there before.

READERS 1, 2 & 3:
UH, FINALLY!

So Long Boots! Who Gives Two Hoots!

A retelling of Peter Johnson's Boots
- A Swedish Tale -
(For **Five Readers**)

READER 1:

Peter Johnson, from all accounts, was a very fortunate man:
Good home, good wife, good pair of boots—a credit to his clan.

READER 2:

But as time went on, poor Peter sang a "hang dog" kind of song;
His shoes—too square, and then too long, too small—everything wrong.

READER 3:

One morning, Peter took a look at the boots which had served for life,
And decided to dispose of them—an impulse that shocked his wife.

PETER:

These boots must go, or I'll turn wacky, my feet are growing roots;
Or perchance the boots have shrunk—about the pair, who gives two hoots?

WIFE:

Sell your boots, your only boots! What's gotten into your head?

PETER:

They've served me well, but I think it's time I had another pair instead.

WIFE:

All I hear is, "Too short," and then they are too long!
Clearly there's a problem—your boots are right, but your head's all wrong.

PETER:

My feet may have grown – or they may have shrunk;
All I know for certain, I'm a miserable old hunk!

There's another thing I'm sure of—something's wrong with this leather!
Well, really two things, that is—I'm at the end of my tether!

READER 1:

So Peter decided to go into town with ten silver coins from his chest;
Even with his wife's disapproval, he knew this was for the best.

READER 2:

Then, to Peter's utter amazement he encountered a man lugging boots;
He was sure this was his chance—jubilant to his roots.

PETER:

Just the man I was looking for, I'd like to propose a trade.

READER 3:

A trade it was, but he gave three bucks to boot;
Still Peter knew he had made the grade.

READER 2:

So he donned his new clogs and merrily went on the beat;
But it wasn't long before he felt a pinching in both feet.

READER 1:

Then Peter met another man; whose boots appeared just right!

PETER:

I'll make an offer, an even trade for your boots which look a bit tight.

READER 2:

The stranger proposed a counter offer—three dollars to boot, or no deal;
Peter knew that even at that, this price was an absolute steal.

READER 3:

Cheerfully he laced his new acquisition, once more he was on his way;
But the moment his weight was on his feet—pinched nerves, to his utter dismay.

PETER:

These boots are the worst I've had so far, I must learn to be more discreet;
I won't give up until I find a pair that hugs my feet.

READER 1:

And voila, he met this fine gentleman; his boots, what a perfect pair!
Peter knew that finally, for sure—he had found boots with flair.

READER 2:

But the stranger was not easily taken; no trade, but a cash deal or "no go!"
Peter handed over his last four bucks, that was the end of his dough.

READER 3:

Peter put on these wonderful boots; no pinching, not a vestige of pain;
Now, indeed, he could walk again, a testament to his fine brain!

READER 1:

When Peter returned to his home he walked on the floor till it creaked;
Proudly he held out his feet, till his wife finally decided to speak.

So Long Boots! Who Gives Two Hoots!

WIFE:

So now you've found the perfect pair, that you're so proudly flaunting;

PETER:

A perfect pair, indeed, I've found—and I do not need your taunting.

WIFE:

Not too narrow, not too short? Not too square in the toes?

PETER:

Oh, what impertinent questions you raise! You think I've paid through the nose.

WIFE:

Not too long, not too pinchy? Really the perfect pair?

PETER:

I've heard enough, turn down the heat! They fit like they're made for my feet.
For a mere ten dollars, a price that is fair; I've found comfort and joy, I declare!

WIFE:

Ten dollars? Ten dollars you paid? I hope you feel some shame!
Turn those boots upside down, and there you'll find one
Peter Johnson's name!

READER 2:

Poor Peter's face showed a sign of shame;
Though his wife bore little long-term resentment;

READER 3:

After all, ten dollars was a meagre price to pay for peace and contentment.

Mandarin Magic

A retelling of Mandarin Duck—A Japanese Tale
(For Six Readers)

READER 1:

> Long ago and far away in the land of the Rising Sun;
> Lived a mandarin duck, and a drake whose plumage was second to none.

READER 2:

> He was adorned in magnificent colours—a coat of the very best;
> His mate was plain, but no doubt, well camouflaged in her nest.

READER 3:

> One day as the drake was foraging, feathers aglow like a brilliant banner,
> His beauty caught the cruel eye of the lord of an exquisite manor.

READER 1:

> The lord ordered one-eyed Shozo to capture the beautiful drake;
> Shozo tried his best to warn him that this could be a terrible mistake.

SHOZO:

> The bird will not survive his capture;
> His spirit will be subdued,
> It might be best to enjoy his beauty
> In the serenity of the wood.

LORD:

> I must adorn my lordly mansion,
> Entice him with acorns on the path;
> I need the plumage now—
> Do my bidding or feel my wrath.

READER 2:

> The drake came through the undergrowth; collected acorns for his brood;
> Forgot all about the lurking dangers while he was gathering food.

READER 3:

> Completely lost in this searching mode, without a thought or care;
> Made him an easy target for the landlord's hidden snare.

READER 1:

The Lord revelled in his rare acquisition—this glorious display of plumage;
He gave orders for a lavish feast, the drake's grandeur at centre stage.

READER 2:

Alas! The memory of his woodland past filled the poor drake with remorse;
His crest soon drooped, he lost his lustre, and his cries were weary and hoarse.

READER 3:

The lord of the manor was displeased and wanted the drake out of sight;
He had no patience for anything that would diminish his great might.

SHOZO:

The bird no longer pleases you; we'll release him if you don't mind;
His spirit may again return when he is with his kind.

LORD:

It's not your duty to suggest without invitation, at least;
I make decisions in this manor—what's best for bird or beast!

READER 1:

And so the drake was simply taken away from public view;
Till, Yasuko, the manor kitchen maid made a decision out of the blue.

READER 2:

In the dead of night, no moon, no stars—when no one was awake,
She took the cage and opened the door and released the weakened drake.

LORD:

Shozo, you traitor, I know that you've stolen my failing drake;
I'm telling you now, you one-eyed liar; you've made a huge mistake.

READER 3:

Shozo would not speak in his defense; hung his head in utter shame;
He had wished freedom for the bird, felt guilt; thus took the blame.

YASUKO:

Dear Shozo, I have to confess
To performing the stealthy release;
Unless I clear you of the blame,
I will never be at peace.

SHOZO:

Dear soul, do not worry
At all about my humiliation;
No need for two to suffer
The lord's venting and degradation.

READER 1:

This truly touching circumstance sparked love with a radiant glow.
The two could not disguise this fact—soon everyone would know.

LORD:

I've become aware of your secrecy—the conspiracy to remove my drake;
You've stretched my merciful nature—my pride as lord is at stake.

READER 2:

There was no doubt now of their fate; the lord had spoken, and his word was law;
Any act construed as deception would forever stick in his craw.

READER 3:

The lord sent for his retainers to dispatch his resolution.
The two were marched immediately to the pond for execution.

READER 1:

But wait! A messenger appeared
With a decree at the royal grounds;
An edict sent by the emperor, proclaiming;
That capital punishment was "out-of-bounds."

READER 2:

This vision from the merciful Buddha reached the remotest villa and port;
All those under the sentence of death were to appear at the Imperial Court.

Mandarin Magic

LORD:

I'm angry at this bizarre decree, I'm used to having my own way;
But what can I possibly do—I am expected to blindly obey.

READER 3:

The march to the Court was a five-day trek;
Hands bound, Yasuko and Shozo lost their way in the darkened night;
Unwittingly, the guards who were to guide them
Had rushed, and by now were way out of sight.

YASUKO:

We're lost, and without food or drink, my mistake is indescribably huge;
If it hadn't been for my foolishness, the warm manor would be our refuge.

SHOZO:

Hush! There's nothing foolish about compassion; please, do not be cross;
Besides, the danger of the forest pales against the cruelty of our boss.

YASUKO:

I would so like to hold your hand, but this binding rope's so tight;
If only we could free ourselves we'd feel safer through the night.

SHOZO:

Come closer to me, Yasuko, so that your shoulder touches mine;
Then we'll never lose each other—I know we'll be just fine.

READER 1:

At that very moment, in the silence of night
Came a sound of rustling leaves—wind-blown;
With baited breath the pair just waited
Like pillars of solid stone.

READER 2:

What a great relief from fear, what a burden off their chest;
They heard faint, soft voices:

VOICES:

We'll provide you with some rest.

READER 3:

The voices again, and once again hidden from sight in the impenetrable night,

VOICES:

We are the Imperial Messengers, come to free you from your plight.

READER 1:

    Yasuko and Shozo, the baffled pair followed in awe and fright;
    Their only lead was the rustling silks in the pitch black dark of night.

READER 2:

    The four arrived in a moonlit clearing—a hut made of grass and slats;
    The messengers took the pair inside; to the comfort of cozy mats.

READER 3:

    They severed the seering tethers,
    Massaged their sore wrists, all blued;
    Each soaked in a large wooden bathtub;
    Deep sighs and murmurs—fresh and renewed.

READER 1:

    Adorned in fresh kimonos, the two elated to be released.
    And to add to the amazing pleasure they partook of a scrumptious feast.

READER 2:

    Tired, and sated with delicious food, one soon heard a unified snore;
    As the two were dreaming in comfort on quilts laid on a tatami floor.

READER 3:

    Yasuko and Shozo woke to the smell of soup and rice, bubbling and steaming;
    No sight of the messengers who had left them while they were still dreaming.

YASUKO:

    We have been thoughtless and rude; we should have thanked those men
    For their kindness and consideration—we may never see them again.

SHOZO:

    I see a Mandarin duck and a gorgeous drake; they seem to be taking a bow.
    As to how we received our freedom—I think I'm getting it now.

READER 1:

    And with that, the ducks flew off to their refuge in the dark green wood;
    Yasuko and Shozo now were sure that freeing the drake had been for the good.

READER 2:

    The two lived happily, and would always remember
    How intimidated they'd been, and scared;
    But mostly they remembered the truth:
    That troubles are eased when they're shared.

Why the Sea is Salt

A retelling of the Norse Tale

(For **Five Readers**)

READER 1:

> King Frodi, wealthy King of the Northland, had a heart for people's needs;
> He was known throughout the land for kindness and kingly deeds.

READER 2:

> Weary travelers would stop to be blessed with the bounty from Frodi's hand;
> It seemed that heaven itself blessed the rich harvests of the land.

READER 3:

> One day the King received a peculiar gift:
> A giant pair of millstones;
> Any attempts to lift them
> Was met with enormous groans.

READER 4:

> While the stones were by no means pretty,
> They soon gained royal attention
> When it was learned that their value
> Exceeded the treasures in the royal mansion.

READER 5:

> These stones had the magical power
> To grind gems of every kind;
> They even granted gifts of love,
> Solace, and peace of mind.

READER 1:

> But, not even the strongest warriors had strength to turn these stones;
> So the King set out in search for folks with muscle and sturdy bones.

READER 2:

> One day as the King was riding, two women of enormous size,
> Baring the widest shoulders and limbs—appeared before his eyes.

READER 3:

There was no time to waste—up front, he'd make no bones;
He invited them to enter the palace and check his enormous millstones.

READERS 1 & 2:

Oh yes,

READER 4:

They answered in one quick breath;

READERS 1 & 2:

To move those stones is no feat;
Tell us what we should grind for you,
It will be done "tout suite."

READER 5:

Gold, grind gold till I can see a massive, glittering mound.
What a pleasure, what a joy—this treasure I have found.

READER 3:

Baring their enormous arms, the women were busying earning their keep.
And in no time at all, there was a glorious, glittering heap.

READER 1:

The King's eyes glistened with glee even as muscles grew weary and sore.
Greed had quickly taken hold as he urged for more and more.

READER 4:

All the women were allowed
Was the odd hurried meal;
How quickly the noble King's heart
Had turned to solid steel.

READER 2:

He had all but forgotten
That the stones could grind gifts of peace;
His heart was set on one thing only:
Like the man with the "golden geese."

Why the Sea is Salt

READER 1:

   The women were exhausted—no recourse but to stop;
   They knew that very soon the two of them would drop.

READER 2:

   While King Frodi fell asleep the women shifted gears;
   They ground out warriors by the thousands, to become Frodi's dreaded fears.

READER 3:

   They carried off the millstones—took them to the beach;
   There was a ship at anchor—soon they were out of reach.

READER 4:

   Merrily they sailed away—the women and some of the men;
   They decided to amuse themselves by turning the stones again.

READER 5:

   The warriors bade them grind some salt, sparkling like a precious gem;
   There were glistening heaps of it—THEN greed took hold of them.

READER 2:

   Even after hours of work, the warriors urged,

ALL:

   "Grind on!"

READER 4:

   The women knew that unless they connived their work would never be done.

READER 1:

   The woman quickly devised a plan,
   Filled every cranny and chink;
   It wasn't long till the salt weighed down.
   They knew the ship would sink.

ALL:

   And there they are, in the bottom of the sea,
   Still grinding heap upon heap;
   Supplying the world with fine crystals
   In the silence of the deep.